D0042203

Making the Most of Life

- From A to Z

ISBN 0-915720-09-4

Presented to:
Dorothy Zimmerman
4052 153rd Ave NW
Williston, ND 58801
By:
19

Making the Most of Life

- From A to Z

LEROY BROWNLOW

BROWNLOW PUBLISHING COMPANY, INC.
P.O. Box 50545
Fort Worth, Texas 76105

Brownlow Gift Books

Flowers That Never Fade
Flowers of Friendship
Flowers for You
Flowers for Mother
A Father's World
Better Than Medicine — A Merry Heart
Making the Most of Life — From A to Z
A Time to Laugh — or Grandpa Was a Preacher
Thoughts of Gold in Words of Silver
With the Good Shepherd
Living With the Psalms
The Story of Jesus
For Love's Sake
Today Is Mine
Leaves of Gold
Young in Heart
Rainbows
Windows
Daybreak
In His Steps
Some Quiet Place
Peace Be With You
The Fruit of the Spirit
The Greatest Thing in the World
The More Years the More Sunshine
University of Hard Knocks

Contents

Foreword

MAKING THE MOST OF LIFE—*From A to Z* is a volume devoted to self-development and the art of becoming a wonderful, successful and happy person. Beginning with A (Aims) and going through Z (Zeal) we have presented in alphabetical arrangement brief studies on the noblest traits and highest aspirations of life, the qualities which lend value to individual acclaim. By these things men live. We believe that the subject matter is as down to earth as man himself who is made of clay, and as practical as his living in a world which challenges the best within him.

The greatest waste in our society is in man himself, which is the consequence of man's failure to appropriate his powers. The sleeping giant lies within each individual — all that is needed is to awake him. This book gives him a nudge and says, "Wake up!"

There is nothing that makes man strong except that which he carries on the inside of himself. As man cultivates the finer qualities, it is then that he makes the most of life and becomes great and happy, strong and successful.

Life is like a seed with possibilities of endless growth. I pick up an acorn and it begins to whisper in my ear: "I will grow and by and by I will become big and strong, and the birds will nest in me. By and by I will furnish shade in the summer for the weary traveler. By and by I will provide fuel to heat man's home in the frozen winter. By and by I will be shelter to those who seek a roof in time of storm."

Then I ask, "Oh! daydreaming little acorn, wilt thou be all this?" And the acorn confidently replies, "Yes, God and I."

— And that's the challenge of living! and that's the combination that meets the challenge — God and I!

That view is exalted in this volume. The Scriptures are quoted freely, together with the poets and philosophers of yesteryears.

We need to get this business of World Improvement down out of cloud-land into the personal and practical region of each person's life; and to this end, this volume was written.

With Lowell I say, "Not failure, but low aim, is crime"; with Emerson I suggest, "Hitch your wagon to a star"; and with Paul I urge, "Press toward the mark."

And in this spirit, I send this volume on its way, entertaining the hope that it contains both facts and inspiration, which will help both young and old to achieve the goal of MAKING THE MOST OF LIFE — *From A to Z.*

LEROY BROWNLOW

Fort Worth, Texas, U. S. A.

A

Aims

TAKE AIM

YEARS ago an accomplished marksman was passing through a community in which he saw evidence of amazing shooting. On barns, on trees, and on fences were many targets with a bullet hole in the exact center of the bull's eye. So he anxiously sought out the marksman who had performed such astounding feats.

In a congratulatory and inquisitive vein he said: "Your shooting beats anything I have ever seen. How did you do it?"

"No trouble at all," replied the marksman, "I shot first and then drew the circles around the holes."

● *Men often aim at nothing and then try to draw the lines of life around accidental marks.* This is why they go in circles around shots they aimlessly call. If I would make the most of life, I must aim.

A few years ago some young men with bows and arrows were shooting at a target. When the arrows of one of them kept hitting the ground, another companion cried out, "Aim higher! Aim higher! Your arrow-head is always pointed to the ground!" The same is true of man. He goes where he points himself.

● *About the most uncomplimentary remark that can be*

made of one is to say, "He lives an aimless life." The weak person rambles or shambles along, but the strong personality is definite in his pursuits and that's why society honors him. The world is quick to pass over one's lapse of memory or errors of judgment; but aimlessness, never. The plans and purposes of a person are an index to his character, especially when viewed in the light of his motives.

● *The supreme incentive for august achievement and lofty living is noble objectives.* We are not apt to drop very low as long as we reach for a star. The stars are above — so keep reaching.

THE POWER OF WHAT MEN WOULD DO

● *It is what man would do — not necessarily what he achieves — that exalts him.*

> 'Tis not what man does which exalts him,
> But what man would do.
>
> — Robert Browning

The Apostle Paul gave witness to the difference between the goal and the achievement in this comment on his own life:

> Brethren, I count not myself to have apprehended: but this one thing I do, forgetting those things which are behind, and reaching forth unto those things which are before, I press toward the mark for the prize of the high calling of God in Christ Jesus.
>
> — Bible, Philippians 3:13,14

So the crime in life is the failure to have a lofty goal rather than the failure to reach it. In writing life's story, remember:

Though thou hast time
But for a line, be that sublime,
Not failure, but low aim, is crime.
— James Russell Lowell

THE GREAT

● *The Greats in every age have been purposeful people.* For instance, the Bible is resplendent with the names of great men who had high and honorable aims in life:

Abraham who "looked for a city which hath foundations, whose builder and maker is God" (Hebrews 11:10).

Moses who "when he was come to years, refused to be called the son of Pharoah's daughter, choosing rather to suffer affliction with the people of God, than to enjoy the pleasures of sin for a season" (Hebrews 11:24,25).

Joshua who said, "Choose you this day whom ye will serve . . . but as for me and my house, we will serve the Lord" (Joshua 24:15).

Jesus who came "to seek and to save that which was lost" (Luke 10:10).

PERSONAL AIMS

Every individual should make a picture of the kind of person he wants to be. After this picture has been thoroughly imprinted on the mind, it becomes the power to mold him into the image he visualizes. I find power in purposing to be the things I seem and to do the things I deem.

Thus let each take definite aim, as follows:

1. *I aim to be a man,* an adult with an open face, big

heart, broad shoulders and a strong backbone. President Garfield said, "I mean to make myself a man; if I succeed at that, I shall succeed in everything else." The Apostle Paul said, "When I was a child, I spake as a child, I thought as a child: but when I became a man, I put away childish things" (I Corinthians 13:11).

This may seem little, but it is a big order with big rewards. It will empower me to go out with head erect and to deserve the world's respect. It will enable me to like myself.

If human frailties should keep me from fully becoming what I aspire to be, there will still be comfort in the thought that I might have become a bum or a brute, if I had not aimed to be a man — that is success.

2. *I aim to be a friend to man.* The Bible says, "As we have therefore opportunity, let us do good unto all men" (Galatians 6:10). This makes life an enchanting experience; so in poetic language, "Let me live in my house by the side of the road and be a friend to man." — Sam Walter Foss.

3. *I aim to be self-reliant,* which necessitates industry, thrift, invention, courage and doggedness. I plan to make a living, stand on my own feet and carry my own weight. This is the law of God: "In the sweat of thy face shalt thou eat bread, till thou return unto the ground" (Genesis 3:19).

4. *I aim to be constructive.* The wise man is a builder (Matthew 7:24). Anybody can tear down.

> It is a good thing to remember,
>   But a better thing to do —
> Always to work with the construction gang,
>   And not with the wrecking crew.

5. *I aim to have God as my only God,* to fear Him "and keep his commandments; for this is the whole duty of man" (Ecclesiastes 12:13). With this relationship I "shall dwell safely, and shall be quiet from fear of evil" (Proverbs 3:24).

6. *I aim to pursue my goals,* looking straight ahead, turning neither "to the right hand nor to the left" (Proverbs 4:25-27).

7. *I aim to keep the barrel loaded and pull the trigger* — otherwise why aim? For "faith, if it hath not works, is dead, being alone" (James 2:17).

B

Belief

NO one wishes to be a second-class person with second-rate accomplishments. But there is a difference between wishing and believing. Many wish for success, but believe they will fail. They simply don't have the faith to climb the ladder of success. They get a rung or two off the ground and doubt will not permit them to go any higher.

Doubt is a negative power. It cripples initiative and cramps energy. It makes failures of us before we even start. When the mind begins to doubt, then it begins to marshal reasons to support its disbelief.

> Our doubts are traitors,
> And make us lose the good we oft might win,
> By fearing to attempt.
>
> — Shakespeare

Our can'ts and excuses are born of doubts; so faith, the positive attitude, will cure us of the Killer-Diseases of Can'titis and Excusitis.

BELIEF DEFINED

● *"Now faith is the substance of things hoped for, the evidence of things not seen"* (Hebrews 11:1). It gives reality or foundation in the mind for the things hoped for, even though the evidence is unseen. It causes a person to feel as if the things were real and to act as if he actually saw them.

He walks not with the eye of physical sight, but rather with the eye of faith — seeing the unseen. "For we walk by faith and not by sight" (II Corinthians 5:7). It was by faith that Moses "endured, as seeing him who is invisible" (Hebrews 11:27).

● *This definition of faith is illustrated in matters other than religion.* If we have occasion to go to Berlin, it is the belief that there is such a place that causes us to act as if it is so. Belief in the integrity of another moves us to act as if it is the truth, even if it is not. Belief that a certain business venture will be profitable motivates us to act as if it is so, though it may not be.

As long as faith continues, whether it is well-founded or ill-founded, it gives reality to that which is believed.

● *Faith is the yardstick by which your portion in life will be measured to you.* "According to your faith be it unto you" (Matthew 9:29).

● *Belief is a flame in the heart;* without it, the spark of life is gone. Nothing is more chilling than doubt. "And they said one to another, Did not our heart burn within us . . ." (Luke 24:32). It was faith that did it.

Faith will give you the substance to live 365 days a year.

POWER TO BECOME AND BE

Belief is the secret of man's becoming and being, conquering and prevailing. William James, the great psychologist, stated that the greatest factor in any undertaking is one's belief.

Belief is the power to:

• *Become a son of God.* "But as many as received him, to them gave he power to become the sons of God, even to them that believe on his name" (John 1:12).

• *Be a faithful son of God.* "Take heed, brethren, lest there be in any of you an evil heart of unbelief in departing from the living God" (Hebrews 3:12).

BELIEF IS POSITIVE

Belief is the positive attitude:

• *Relative to God* — "I know whom I have believed, and am persuaded that he is able to keep that which I have committed unto him against that day" (II Timothy 1:12).

When darkness fills the sky,
I know by faith we two
Shall win in the end —
My God and I.

With God's help new hopes can replace disappointments; and with faith I can repair my battered ships and send them out again to return fully laden.

I will not doubt, though all my ships at sea
Come drifting home with broken masts and sails;
I shall believe the Hand which never fails
From seeming evil worketh good for me;
And though I weep because those sails are battered,
Still will I cry, while my best hope lies shattered,
"I trust in Thee."

— Ella Wheeler Wilcox

2. *Relative to others* — "Let each esteem other better than themselves" (Philippians 2:3).

Men are good, men are bad, they are weak, they are strong,
 Wise, foolish — so am I.
Hence, I can have more faith in others,
 If I'll just take a look at my own eye.

"And why beholdest thou the mote that is in thy brother's eye, but considerest not the beam that is in thine own eye?" (Matthew 7:3).

3. *Relative to self* — "I can do all things through Christ which strengtheneth me" (Philippians 4:13). Believe in yourself and humanity will believe in you. Doubt yourself and humanity will doubt you. Don't let any person tell you what you "can't do." Dryden said, "For they can conquer who believe they can."

I knew a man who for years was what you call a "one gallus" farmer. Then one day he sat down and began to face up to himself. He took a look at his good and bad points. He had many excellent characteristics necessary to success: intelligence, honesty, integrity, dependability and clean personal habits. But some of his friends with no more of these traits than he were running off and leaving him. What was wrong? For the first time he admitted to himself that he lacked faith. Doubt had stripped him of initiative. His successful friends had faith. After hours of wrestling with himself he decided he would believe in himself, act positively, shake off his chains and go free. He said, "If I'm going to quit playing the role of Doubting Thomas, then I should test myself in the most profitable business in the world." So he quit farming and went into the oil business. A few years ago he died a millionaire.

I am not implying that becoming a millionaire necessarily

makes one a success; but I am contending that belief in yourself is essential to doing things.

FAITH IS THE VICTORY

● *"And this is the victory that overcometh the world, even our faith"* (I John 5:4). Faith is the heroic attitude that sets men apart from the ordinary. The things that distinguished the great men of the Bible from their fellowmen and handed their names down to posterity was faith. By faith they outdid themselves (Hebrews 11).

With faith in God, in others and in self, we can say:

Let the howlers howl, and the growlers growl, and the
  Prowlers prowl, and the gossipers go it;
Behind the night there is plenty of light, and things
  Are all right and — I know it.

C

Courage

ONLY the valiant can make the most of life. Sydney Smith said, "A great deal of talent is lost to the world for the want of a little courage." Fear of failure is the father of failure. The main battlefield is in the heart and the chief foe is Fear.

> I find no foeman in the road but Fear;
> To doubt is failure and to dare success.
>
> — Frederic Lawrence Knowles

● *What a man thinks and does when things are at their worst makes or breaks him.* Crushed hopes, broken trust and bitter disappointment precipitate a crisis for every soul; and it is his behavior then that determines his failure or success. The coward in time of crisis thinks with his legs; but the brave keeps on fighting though he is scared half to death.

● *Men have lacked wisdom on many great issues, because they lacked the courage to be wise.* Through cowardice they chose the way of stupidity, because it was the way of least resistance. Emerson said, "Half a man's wisdom goes with his courage."

Control your fears! For fear is more hurtful than the thing you fear. "Fear makes the wolf bigger than he is." — German Adage. The world awards the best only to men and women of courage.

GOD'S WILL

It is God's will that his children be courageous:

> Be strong and of a good courage, fear not, nor be afraid of them: for the Lord thy God, he it is that doth go with thee: he will not fail thee, nor forsake thee.
>
> — Deuteronomy 31:6

> Let not your heart be troubled, neither let it be afraid.
>
> — John 14:27

> For God hath not given us the spirit of fear; but of love, and of a sound mind [discipline, A.S.V.].
>
> — II Timothy 1:7

KINDS OF COURAGE

Here are some of the kinds of mettle men and women have been called upon to manifest:

1. *Military courage,* the spirit to wield the sword. When the mob came to arrest Jesus, Peter "drew his sword, and struck a servant of the high priest, and smote off his ear" (Matthew 26:51).

2. *Moral courage.* But Peter who had been brave with a sword turned fearful in a moral struggle and denied his Lord thrice (Matthew 26:69-75). This proves that it takes more courage to fight without a sword than it does with it. Through moral stamina we save ourselves from being enslaved.

> They are slaves who will not choose
> Hatred, scoffing and abuse,
> Rather than in silence shrink
> From the truth they needs must think;
> They are slaves who dare not be
> In the right with two or three.
>
> — James Russell Lowell

3. *Business courage.* The one-talent man in the Bible failed because of his fear of losing. His sorrowful comment was: "I was afraid, and went and hid thy talent in the earth" (Matthew 25:25).

4. *Social heroism.* It is easy to stand when the crowd is with you; but it takes backbone to endure the slurs and sneers of fun-makers. Many who can stand up to guns fall before grins. Bullets they can face, but mockery — No! But Nehemiah, who rebuilt the walls of Jerusalem, could. His enemies taunted him with such ridicule: "Even that which they build, if a fox go up, he shall even break down their stone wall" (Nehemiah 4:3). But he endured it and succeeded.

5. *Courage to speak.* Remember — there is "a time to keep silence and a time to speak" (Ecclesiastes 3:7). Some talk valiantly until valor is needed, like a little dog I had which was a terror in chasing a big dog until the big dog stopped — brave until bravery was needed.

6. *Silent fearlessness.* Jesus exemplified this gallantry in refusing to answer the false accusations against him, for their minds were fixed. A sign of a coward is to strive to seem brave. Weaklings boast, brag and swagger. But the bravest bravery is quiet.

7. *Daily and dutiful courage* (Romans 12:1). A higher heroism is to fill a little place because God wills it; to go on cheerfully in a round of little duties; to accept without murmur a low position; to smile for the joys of others when your heart is breaking. He who does this for a lifetime is a greater hero than he who for one hour storms a beach, or for one day rushes in the flaming front of shot and shell. Because no drums beat and no crowds shout a welcome, the heroics of such living is not lessened.

8. *Courage to die for a principle or a cause.* The brave — like Esther and Jesus — have defied death for things which meant more than life. Read Esther 4:15 and John 10:11.

DEVELOPING COURAGE

Here are some factors which militate for courage:

- *Experience has taught us that most of our fears were only imaginary.* As the Psalmist said, "There were they in great fear, where no fear was" (Psalms 53:5). How often our hearts have been in fright at evils which never came in sight.

- *Time has also taught us that many of the things we feared were blessings in disguise.* The trials and struggles of Joseph were necessary steps on the way to a place of renown in the Egyptian government.

> The clouds ye so much dread
> Are big with mercy and shall break
> With blessings on your head.
>
> — William Cowper

- *Right will eventually win.* When right is dungeoned and wrong is enthroned, it is easy to lose courage. But no question is ever settled until it is settled right. Though the enemy seems to have won, just remember —the battle is not yet done. Tomorrow will bring another day.

- *A clear conscience.* "The wicked flee when no man pursueth: but the righteous are bold as a lion" (Proverbs 28:1). "Thus conscience doth make cowards of us all." — Shakespeare.

- *Trust in God is a safeguard from fear.* "But whoso

hearkeneth unto me shall dwell safely, and shall be quiet from fear of evil" (Proverbs 1:33).

● *We increase courage by facing the things we fear and by conquering them.* The secret is found in Paul's statement. "I have fought a good fight" (II Timothy 4:7). The harder he fought, the stronger his courage became.

Do you fear the force of the wind,
The slash of the rain?
Go face them and fight them,
Be savage again.
Go hungry and cold like the wolf,
Go wade like the crane:
The palms of your hands will thicken,
The skin of your cheek will tan,
You'll grow ragged and weary and swarthy,
But you'll walk like a man!

— Hamlin Garland

CONCLUSION

"Be sure you are right and then stand. At first you will be denounced, then you will be deified. At first you will be rejected, then you will be accepted. First men will swear at you, then if you wear well, they will swear by you. First the sneer and then the cheer. First the lash, then the laurel. First the curse, then the caress. First the trial, then the triumph. First the cross, then the crown. For every scar upon thy brow thou shalt have a star in thy diadem. Stand somewhere and let humanity know where you stand. Stand for something and let humanity know what you stand for. Be sure you are right and then STAND!" — Gordon.

D

Diligence

MIGHTY effort will open the door to kings. "Seest thou a man diligent in his business? he shall stand before kings" (Proverbs 22:29) — before rulers, and also kings of finance, education, respect and honor.

THE MOTHER OF GOOD FORTUNE

● *Good fortune demands Aims, Belief and Courage;* but these three would be in vain without the fourth, *Diligence.* Strong characters have wills; feeble ones, only wishes. Diligence is that industrious trait which is always attentive, active and indefatigable, which stands opposed to indifference, carelessness and laziness.

Perhaps you have read in story books the fictitious anecdote of the race between the rabbit and the turtle. The rabbit was quick and swift; the turtle, slow and clumsy. But the turtle possessed one thing the rabbit did not have — diligence. The fleet rabbit would run awhile and nap awhile, but the slow-footed turtle kept plodding along; and while the rabbit dozed, the turtle came in first. The moral is: Victory does not always go to the fastest and most talented, but rather to the most diligent.

The heights by great men — reached and kept —
Were not attained by sudden flight —
But they while their companions slept
Were toiling upward through the night.

— Longfellow

A few days ago I was visiting in the country. I passed one ranch with good barns, strong fences, improved grasses and excellent cattle. Then I passed a run-down spread with dilapidated buildings, deteriorating fences and brushy pastures. Fortune and misfortune — one man gained it and another missed it — because diligence had moved the hand of one and indifference had paralyzed the hand of the other.

● *Aspiration points us, but perspiration gets us there.* Give me the man who aspires and perspires — he will get the job done! No other will!

● *If you would enter the world of good things —*

Don't lazily sit in a boat
That's pushed out to float
And carelessly drift and drift;
But grab an oar and head for the shore
And a land of good things will be yours.

— L. B.

DEFEATING POWER OF SLOTHFULNESS

● *Slothfulness is sure to cut short the expectations of life.* "The slothful man roasteth not that which he took in hunting: but the substance of a diligent man is precious" (Proverbs 12:27). The slothful man is like iron which rusts from disuse; like water which stagnates from stillness.

Several years ago a sheep rancher in Texas hired a man to tend his sheep. But the shepherd carelessly let the sheep get away from him one by one. After three or four months he came into town to see his employer and said, "You are going to have to get me some more sheep to herd; I've run out of sheep." Well! Lots more "running out" occurred — but not sheep!

BUSINESS DILIGENCE

The Bible emphasizes in strong words the need of business diligence:

- *Slothfulness is prohibited* — "Not slothful in business" (Romans 12:11).

- *Work or starve* — "If any would not work, neither should he eat" (II Thessalonians 3:10).

- *Know the state or condition of your enterprise* — "Be thou diligent to know the state of thy flocks, and look well to thy herds" (Proverbs 27:23).

- *The diligent becomes rich* — "He becometh poor that dealeth with a slack hand: but the hand of the diligent maketh rich" (Proverbs 10:4).

- *The ant is used as an example to teach man* — "Go to the ant, thou sluggard; consider her ways and be wise . . . Provideth her meat in the summer, and gathereth her food in the harvest" (Proverbs 6:6-8).

DOMESTIC DILIGENCE

- *Failure to provide for one's own is a denial of the faith* — "But if any provide not for his own, and specially for those of his own house, he hath denied the faith, and is worse than an infidel" (I Timothy 5:8).

- *The model woman* — "riseth also while it is yet night, and giveth meat to her household" (Proverbs 31:15). "She eateth not the bread of idleness" (Proverbs 31:27).

RELIGIOUS DILIGENCE

The Bible also demands diligence in spiritual matters:

• *The heart is to be kept diligently* — "Keep thy heart with all diligence; for out of it are the issues of life" (Proverbs 4:23).

• *Christ knew the value of working today* — "I must work the works of him that sent me, while it is day: the night cometh, when no man can work" (John 9:4).

• *No season permits indifference* — "Be instant in season, out of season" (II Timothy 4:2).

• *Diligence is required to make calling and election sure* — "Give diligence to make your calling and election sure" (II Peter 1:10).

• *There is no escape for those who neglect* — "How shall we escape, if we neglect so great salvation?"

• *Be diligent to be blameless* — "Be diligent that ye may be found of him in peace, without spot, and blameless" (II Peter 3:14).

• *Stay ready* — "And they that were ready went in with him to the marriage: and the door was shut" (Matthew 25:10).

IN CONCLUSION, we say:

> Bite off more than you can chew and chew it;
> Plan more than you can do and do it;
> Hitch your wagon to a star,
> Keep your seat — and there you are.

E

Endurance

I KNOW a great and successful man who teaches a Bible class in the church where he is a member. His favorite text is this one sentence:

> They went forth to go into the land of Canaan; and into the land of Canaan they came.
>
> — Genesis 12:5

One of the essentials in making the most of life is to *have some aims* to which we start — "They went forth to go into the land of Canaan." Another is to *keep on going* after we start — "Into the land of Canaan they came."

This verse has meant much to this man of Aims, Belief, Courage, Determination and Endurance.

VOICES OF NATURE

Shakespeare said, "Our life . . . finds tongues in trees, books in running brooks, sermons in stones, and good in everything."

Lumbermen and scientists who examined a big tree in California after it had been cut down found that it began growing 271 years before the birth of Christ. When it was 516 years old it was partly burned, the charted portions of the bark and trunk being visible far inside the giant. Other fires left their marks upon it in 1441, 1580 and 1797. The latter made an enormous scar eighteen feet wide.

That tree is a lesson in patient endurance in overcoming

obstacles! Burned, disfigured and partly destroyed, each time it covered up its wounds, broadened out and continued its reach toward the sky. The good persevering man is "like a tree planted by the rivers of water . . ." (Psalms 1:3).

Two little brooks start their journey to the ocean, hoping to supply fresh sparkling water to the people along the way and desiring to furnish the life-sustaining power to trees and grass and flowers beside its banks. One endures and the other dries up.

The diamond is just a piece of coal that stuck to its job.

Even the little spider has been used in the Bible to teach man an illustrative lesson: "The spider taketh hold with her hands, and is in king's palaces" (Proverbs 30:28). A man who was forced to take shelter in a barn fixed his eyes upon a spider climbing a beam of the room. It fell to the ground twelve consecutive times, but succeeded the thirteenth time and gained the top.

● *Nature tells us that the best in life never comes easily,* but rather is so protected as to be denied us unless challenged by perseverance. The rose is guarded by its thorns and honey is defended by the bees; so no person can have either who is annoyed by briers or discouraged by the fear of being stung.

THE BIBLE

Here are some passages from the Bible which teach man how to live the successful life by laying down the absolute necessity of endurance:

> No man, having put his hand to the plow, and looking back, is fit for the kingdom of God.
>
> — Luke 9:62

But he that shall endure unto the end, the same shall be saved.

— Mark 13:13

Be not overcome of evil, but overcome evil with good.

— Romans 12:21

Be ye steadfast, unmovable, always abounding in the work of the Lord, forasmuch as ye know that your labor is not in vain in the Lord.

— I Corinthians 15:58

Be thou faithful unto death, and I will give thee a crown of life.

— Revelation 2:10

This iron-like quality is so important that the Bible employs some of the most graphic and analogical language in describing the failure to maintain it — like "The dog [that] is turned to his own vomit again; and the sow that was washed to her wallowing in the mire" (II Peter 2:22).

PROVERBS

This quality that we sometimes call *stickability* is so vital that men have applauded its greatness in the creation of proverbs:

One may go far after he is tired.

— French

With time a mulberry leaf becomes satin.

— Chinese

We will see who can pound the longest.

— Wellington at Waterloo

The secret of winning is in lasting longer than the other fellow.

— L. B.

You can lengthen your sword by adding a step to it.

— L. B.

The road to success has its ups and downs but no stops.

— L. B.

Stick to your aim; the mongrel's hold will slip,
But only crow-bars loose the bulldog's grip;
Small as he looks, the jaw that never yields
Drags down the bellowing monarch of the fields.

— Oliver Wendell Holmes

POWERFUL PEOPLE

● *All effectual lives have had in common the genius of endurance.* Success does not come without its setbacks. To be on the right road is not enough — we must travel it. It will not suffice to begin well; we must end well. Paul began ill but ended well; Judas began well but ended ill! All great people have had an extra portion of staying power:

1. *Moses* — "For he endured, as seeing him who is invisible" (Hebrews 11:27).

2. *Job* in his afflictions — "Till I die I will not remove mine integrity from me. My righteousness I hold fast, and will not let it go" (Job 27:5,6).

3. *Jesus* on the cross — "It is finished" (John 11:30).

4. *Paul* at the close of life — "I have fought a good fight, I have finished my course, I have kept the faith" (II Timothy 4:7). For a description of his endurance record read II Corinthians 11:23-27.

5. *Edison* — His storage-battery invention was the result of nine thousand experiments. But to succeed was worth 8,999 temporary failures.

6. *Gibbon* — Worked twenty years on *The Decline and Fall of the Roman Empire.*

7. *Cyrus Field* — In giving his account of the Atlantic telegraph, said: "It has been a long and hard struggle. Nearly thirteen years of anxious watching and ceaseless toil. Often has my heart been ready to sink. Many times . . . I have almost accused myself of madness and folly to sacrifice the peace of my family, and all the hopes of life, for what might prove, after all, but a dream. I have seen my companions one after another fall by my side, and I feared I, too, might not live to see the end. And yet one hope has led me on."

8. *Columbus* — Here is a poetic tribute to him and a commendation of the lesson he gave us to go on and on:

"My men grow mutinous day by day;
My men grow ghostly wan and weak."
The stout mate thought of home; a spray
Of salt wave washed his swarthy cheek.
"What shall I say, brave Admiral, say,
If we sight naught but seas at dawn?"
"Why, you shall say at break of day;
'Sail on! sail on! sail on! and on!' "

They sailed. They sailed. Then spoke the mate:
"This mad sea shows its teeth tonight,
He curls his lip, he lies in wait,
With lifted teeth, as if to bite!
Brave Admiral, say but one good word,
What shall we do when hope is gone?"
The words leapt as a leaping sword,
"Sail on! sail on! sail on! and on!"

Then, pale and worn, he kept his deck,
And peered through darkness. Ah, that night
Of all dark nights! And then a speck —
A light! A light! A light!
It grew, a starlit flag unfurled!
It grew to be Times's burst of dawn:
He gained a world; he gave that world
Its grandest lesson: "On and on!"

— Joaquin Miller

F

Forgiveness

IT happened in a little church, in a little town. I was there; I saw it; I heard it. Toward the conclusion of the service, a trembling woman came forward and sat on the front pew, asking forgiveness. She had been an absenter for several years. The woman who sat directly behind her, shocked, grew pale and nervous. Several in the audience seemed bewildered and wondered if trouble would start all over again; for there had been trouble, lots of it, tragic and heart-breaking — two murders, court trials with opposing families, and one death in the electric chair.

The responding woman was the mother of the murderer. The woman behind her . . . it was her husband and son whose blood had been shed. What will her reaction be? Will her mercy go unstrained? Will her forgiveness be big enough to welcome the mother of the man who widowed her and left her bereft of both husband and son? It was! She went to her, clasped her hand, and said, "I'm glad you have come back to be with us in the church." She later commented, "I feel better than I have felt in years. Now I feel free."

● *"Now I feel free"* — an expression of a liberating principle in the art of living! One may be imprisoned while he is free or be free while he is in prison, depending upon how he binds or looses himself within his own heart.

Amidst the fabulous wealth of Egypt and the glory and

splendor of royalty, nervousness paced the second ruling power in the land as emotion pulled at his heart strings. But like sunshine suddenly darting through breaking clouds, a sigh of relief went up at the announcement: "Joseph, it is a boy!" He named that son *Manasseh;* "For God, said he, hath made me forget all my toil, and all my father's house" (Genesis 41:51). Forgiveness!

What had he forgotten? The unmerciful abuse of his envious brothers who sold him into slavery; his servitude in Potiphar's house; the lies of a lustful, conniving, vengeful woman that sent him to prison. Now it is different — now he is on top! And the secret of the climb was his own forgiving spirit. He could have chained and shackled himself with rancor and retaliation, vindictiveness and vengeance — many have! But he didn't! He enjoyed the only real freedom there is, *freedom within;* so he was free to rise — and he did!

Stone walls do not a prison make,
  Nor iron bars a cage.
Minds innocent and quiet take
  That for a hermitage.

— Richard Lovelace

But —

If my soul is devoid of love —
  Forgive others? No! It's just for me —
Hate bound, no cooing of the dove,
  Imprisoned, I've lost my liberty.

— L. B.

THREEFOLD FORGIVENESS

Inasmuch as sin is common to man (I John 1:8), we shall ever be called upon to face the problem of imperfection and the need of forgiveness:

1. *Forgiveness from God* — "Our Father which art in heaven . . . forgive us our debts" (Matthew 6:9-12).

2. *Forgiveness of others* — ". . . as we forgive our debtors" (Matthew 6:12).

3. *Forgiveness of self* — "Forgetting those things which are behind" (Philippians 3:13). Paul forgave himself and reached forth unto better things. The only way to judge a man's religion is by what it does — "the tree is known by its fruits" (Matthew 12:33). If your religion does not have roots deep enough to tap God and his fruit-bearing power and, in return, produce the godly fruit of forgiveness, then it is too shallow to be worth very much.

THE BIGNESS OF FORGIVENESS

It is:

- *Understanding* — "Father, forgive them; for they know not what they do" (Luke 23:34).

- *Merciful* — "Then the Lord of that servant was moved with compassion, and loosed him, and forgave him the debt" (Matthew 18:27).

- *Forgetful* — "And their sins and iniquities will I remember no more" (Hebrews 10:17).

- *Numberless* — "How oft shall my brother sin against me, and I forgive him? . . . . . Not . . . until seven times: but, until seventy times seven" (Matthew 18:21, 22).

- *Helpful* like the sandal tree that perfumes the axe that lays it low — "Bless them that curse you, and do good to them that hate you, and pray for them which despitefully use you, and persecute you" (Matthew 5:44)

● *God-like* — "For thou, Lord, art good, and ready to forgive" (Psalms 86:5).

INDUCEMENTS TO FORGIVE

● *It is the wronged person's glory to forgive* — "The discretion of a man deferreth his anger; and it is his glory to pass over a transgression" (Proverbs 19:11). Forgiveness distinguishes big and little people — only the big and brave can practice it.

> Generous and magnanimous minds are readiest to forgive; and it is a weakness and impotency of mind to be unable to forgive.
>
> — Lord Bacon

● *The good life cannot go on without forgiving and forgetting.* Bury the past and, as Spurgeon said, "When you bury a mad dog, don't leave his tail above the ground."

● *An awareness of how much I need forgiveness makes me more tolerant of the other fellow* (Matthew 7:3). Unfortunately those who are guilty of the same wrong find it harder to forgive others. It is what psychology calls *projection;* it is their way of fighting or hiding their own sin.

● *A conviction that God will not forgive me unless I forgive others encourages this God-like goodness* — "If ye forgive not men their trespasses, neither will your Father forgive your trespasses" (Matthew 6:15)

● *A practical view of live* — a recognition of humanity's fallibility and goodness — urges clemency. Richard Baxter, in his old age, put it this way:

> I see that good men are not as good as I once thought they were, and find that few men are as bad as their enemies imagine.

• *A meditative stroll through the cemetery,* as John Greenleaf Whittier stated, helps one to forgive:

> . . . I strolled among
> The green mounds of the village burial-place;
> Where, pondering how all human love and hate
> Find one sad level . . .
> Awed for myself, and pitying my race, depart,
> Our common sorrow, like a mighty wave,
> Swept all my pride away, and, trembling, I forgave!

G

Growth

WHAT is this thing called *Life* all about? Briefly, it is progression or retrogression, development or disintegration. The irrevocable law of God demands that we make the most of life, *keep on growing — or die!* The two great laws of life are growth and death. When things stop growing they start dying. This is true of vegetation, animals, humans, businesses, churches and nations.

Plants, animals and people grow until they become grown and then death gradually commences; this is the climax and the anti-climax of growth. But there is one type of growth in which this need not be true — the growth *within* a person, beautifully stated by the Apostle Paul:

> For which cause we faint not; but though our outward man perish, yet the inward man is renewed day by day.
>
> — II Corinthians 4:16

Early life involves replacing outgrown clothing; and adult life consists of replacing worn-out erasers, abolishing illusions and discarding errors — but there is no other way to grow. Every good thing is obtained at the expense of giving up something else.

● *We can't go to a Finishing School and get finished.* Nature exacts more of us than this. The whole world is the Finishing School and the course lasts from the cradle to the grave; and we should not consider ourselves finished until death comes.

● *Growth is the "Harp of a Thousand Strings"* where — and only where — the raptures of an infinite gladness may be played. Growth gives melody to life; but retardation fills it with discord. Happy people are living, growing people; the unhappy ones died a long time ago.

The gratification that you are growing drives out the gloom that comes from a sense of shortcoming. As long as you are growing, you are not failing. Growth implies imperfection all right, that you have not yet arrived, but it also signifies improvement. The Apostle Paul worded it this way:

> I count not myself to have apprehended... and reaching forth unto those things which are before, I press toward the mark for the prize...
>
> — Philippians 3:13,14

NATURE TEACHES GROWTH

● *Nature has a voice which says, "Grow!"* As Shakespeare stated, there are "tongues in trees," and "books in running brooks."

When Longfellow was old, an enthusiastic admirer asked him how it was that he was able to keep so vigorous and write so beautifully. Pointing to a tree clothed in blooms, the aged poet replied: "That apple tree is very old, but I never saw prettier blossoms upon it than those it now bears. The tree grows a little new wood every year, and I suppose it is out of that new wood that those blossoms come. Like the apple tree, I try to grow a little new wood every year."

O that I may grow!
I see the leaves out-pushing hour by hour,
With steady joy the buds burst out a flower,
Urged gladly on by Nature's working power.
O that I may grow!

— Maltbie Davenport Babcock

THE BIBLE TEACHES GROWTH

The Bible, a book on the science of right living, holds forth growth:

A COMMAND — "As newborn babes, desire the sincere milk of the word, that ye may grow thereby" (I Peter 2:2).

JESUS EXPERIENCED A FOURFOLD GROWTH at the age of twelve — "and Jesus increased in wisdom [intellectually] and stature [physically], and in favor with God [religiously] and man [socially]" (Luke 2:52).

THE THESSALONIANS WERE GROWING IN FAITH AND LOVE — "Your faith groweth exceedingly, and the charity of every one of you all toward each other aboundeth" (II Thessalonians 1:3).

BE STRONGER AND STRONGER is God's plan for us — "The righteous also shall hold on his way, and he that hath clean hands shall be stronger and stronger" (Job 17:9).

PENALTIES FOR NOT GROWING

Nature assesses a severe penalty for those who fail to grow:

● *In Intellectualism — they die above the ears;* lose zest; dry up a thousand streams of knowledge and inspiration which could refresh their lives and invite old age before their time. You may take off some of the dullness of life by becoming sharper.

• *In business — the symied are stuck with the lesser positions;* even more hurtful, like the one-talent man, they stand a good chance to lose what they have (Matthew 25:28). The business world says to all who enter her gates: "Produce — or be cut down, like the fig tree in the Bible" (Luke 13:6,7).

• *In sociability — the sociably retarded lose the warmth of friends and the strength of fellowship.* Jesus was friendly and sociable with everyone who would permit it. One of the beautiful attributes of the early church is they broke "bread from house to house" (Acts 2:46). The world is wanting to clasp the hand of friendship; keep yours extended if you would have friends. "A man that hath friends must how himself friendly" (Proverbs 18:24).

• *In spirituality* — (1) the spiritually stunted are hindered from "laying aside all malice, and all guile, the hypocrisies, and envies, and all evil speakings" (I Peter 2:1); (2) they are stopped in adding the Christian graces: knowledge, temperance, patience, godliness, brotherly kindness, and love (II Peter 1:5-7); and (3) like branches cut from the vine, they will be severed from the Lord (John 15:6).

"Blessed are the dead who die {physically} in the Lord" (Revelation 14:13), but cursed are the living who die in stagnation!

A MAN

"What a man!" we exclaim as we look upon the powerful physique of the athlete. He may be! But neither the scales nor the yardstick will reveal it. Bring in your measurements that give the size of his mind and soul — then we shall know! Isaac Watts, who was only five feet tall, composed at the moment this reply to an annoyer who teased him about his small stature:

> Were I so tall to reach the pole,
> Or grasp the ocean with my span,
> I must be measured by my soul:
> The mind's the standard of the man.

May each be able to say, "When I become a man, I put away childish things" (I Corinthians 13:11); and may each continue to grow.

> What thought Time cuts his furrows in my face,
> My heart may ever add grace unto grace,
> Graces with added days still keeping pace,
> O that I may grow!
>
> — Maltbie Davenport Babcock

Yes! Though time cuts furrows in my face, may I ever grow and be fruitful.

> The righteous shall flourish like the palm tree...
> They shall still bring forth fruit in old age.
>
> — Psalms 92:12-14

Hope

Hope deferred maketh the heart sick, but when the desire cometh, it is a tree of life.

— Solomon, Ecclesiastes 13:12

WE say of this one or that one, "He has lost heart." What we really mean is, "He has lost hope." When hope gets sick and dies, man becomes sick at heart; and life becomes empty because his dreams have expired and his purposes for living have stopped pulsating. So when hope is gone, all is gone — nothing is left. But where hope is, there is POWER OF LIFE:

- *Hope is the medicine that prevents heart-sickness and the tree that produces life.* There is no tonic as potent as the hope that tomorrow will be better; and there is no tree as fruitful as good things desired and expected.

- *Hope is also an anchor:*

Which hope we have as an anchor of the soul, both sure and steadfast.

— Hebrews 6:19

And when the storm rages, and when engines, compass and steering gear fail, sailors may still hope in the anchor. Likewise, it is hope which anchors us poor, weather-beaten, storm-tossed seamen when everything else is swept from us. And just as long as hope holds, just that long we can be sure and steadfast and hold our moorings.

● *Hope is the moving force behind man's activities.* Sophocles stated: "It is hope which maintains most of mankind." Our world is one of hope. Martin Luther philosophized: "Everything that is done in the world is done by hope." The Bible says:

> . . . he that ploweth should plow in hope; and that he that thresheth in hope should be partaker of his hope.
>
> I Corinthians 9:10

Hope of a crop prompts the farmer to drive the plow; hope of a victory urges the soldier to fight; hope of oil causes the wildcatter to drill; hope of winning makes the athlete run; and hope of the incorruptible crown inspires the child of God to run in the race of life (I Corinthians 9:24-26).

● *Hope is a dynamic, triumphant power.* It — "I know . . . and am persuaded" attitude — sustained the Apostle Paul in all his distressing experiences. Hear him: "We are troubled on every side, yet not distressed; we are perplexed, but not in despair; persecuted, but not forsaken; cast down, but not destroyed" (II Corinthians 4:8,9). He knew, with God's help, he was bigger than the things that were trying to down him. To the person of hope, difficulties are only opportunities for him to show his power; problems, the laboratory to try his skill in their solution; and thunder-clouds, the canvas on which to paint the pictures of his unrealized ambitions. *Hope never says fail!*

> In life's earnest battle they only prevail
> Who daily march onward, and never say fail.

● *Hope is a gladdening power* — "The hope of the righteous shall be gladness" (Proverbs 10:28). Some things go together like hope and gladness. It is through hope that man expects a blessing out of every calamity. Hope sees a star and the world brightens up. "The sun sets; but not his hope: Stars rose; his faith was earlier up." —Ralph Waldo Emerson.

● *Hope is the pillow of assurance for weary heads.* The Bible speaks of "the full assurance of hope" (Hebrews 6:11). A soft pillow for a night's repose — that is rest! As the evening shadows gather, it is through hope — desire and expectation — that I can pray God to forgive and keep my life, as expressed by Harriet McEwen Kimball:

> The day is ended. Ere I sink to sleep,
> My weary spirit seeks repose in Thine.
> Father! forgive my trespasses, and keep
> This little life of mine.

HOW HOPE IS OBTAINED

1. *As long as there is life, there is hope.* "For to him that is joined to all the living there is hope: for a living dog is better than a dead lion" (Ecclesiastes 9:4).

2. *There is hope in God:* "And now, Lord, what wait I for? my hope is in thee" (Psalms 39:7). It gives the world a new look. It gives one courage to —

> Do thy duty; that is best;
> Leave unto the Lord the rest.
>
> — James Russell Lowell

3. *Hope is obtained through the Scriptures* — ". . . that we through patience and comfort of the Scriptures might have hope" (Romans 15:4). Read them to know, and believe them to hope.

4. *It gives hope to realize that your difficulties are only the common lot of man;* others have them, too, and they presevere — so can you!

Don't think your lot the worst because
Some griefs your joy assail;
There aren't so very many saws
That never strike a nail.

— Nixon Waterman

But hopeful carpenters file the saw and keep on building houses; and when men of hope see their plans strike a snag, they smooth the broken places and keep on building castles.

5. *Experience has given us hope.* "Tribulation worketh patience; and patience, experience; and experience, hope" (Romans 5:3,4). Trial or proving has been a great teacher which has taught us that most troubles never occur; and the ones that do, can someway be handled.

6. *Our greatest cause for hope is the assurance of eternal life* (Titus 3:7), and without it "we are of all men most miserable" (I Corinthians 15:19). If in this life you lose and lose and lose, remember: you can enter another life in which you are sure to win and win and win — and never lose.

ON TOP THE WORLD

In the Tate Gallery in London is Frederic Watt's famous painting, *Hope.* There is a delicate, lovely woman seated upon a globe. Her head is bowed and her eyes are blindfolded, as if stricken and dejected. She holds in her hand a harp with only one string, which is stretched to the snapping point — all others have already broken; and her hand touches that one string — hope — and, with head bent toward it to catch the melody, she plays music, sweet, soulful and satisfying. In that simple and profound presentation there is pathos and tenderness. When your little world stops turning and your own personal sun quits shining, how wonderful that hope can take up life's harp and play upon the one remaining string. When you can do that, there is still a chance for you.

I

Influence

MY friend, the minister, walked with the condemned man down Death Row in an Oklahoma Penitentiary. The sunshine friends who had exploited the doomed man in fair weather had disappeared like shadows at the approach of clouds. But he had found a friend in a man he had never known before, a man who loved him only for what he was, a creature in the image of God — not for what he could get out of him! Here we see two influences — one that had undone him, and another that was trying to tie him back together again. That is where man lives — between good and bad influences.

It was a brief walk; but actually it was a long walk that began years before! That man had once been a good church member, the salt of the earth. But something went wrong. Something caused him to drop beneath himself. What was it? Influence! The influence of a woman who used several dollars worth of dope everyday. Her financial demands were too great for a laboring man; so it was not long until the poor man worked all the day and stole half the night. He was caught, tried and sent to the penitentiary. In prison, he became bitter; hate ate him up on the inside. After his release, like a tracking animal pursuing its prey, he hunted the man he thought had "sent him up" and shot him down in cold-blooded murder. This time, the court's penalty was death, a life for a life.

While this is an extreme case, it is not unusual for lives, careers and souls to be saved or lost through influence. It is a big word in making the most of life! It can fan a flame or blow it out.

A BREATH

A breath can fan love's flame to burning,
Make firm resolve of trembling doubt,
But, strange! at fickle fancy's turning,
The selfsame breath can blow it out.

— Mary Ainge DeVere

BE CAUTIOUS IN CHOOSING ASSOCIATES

● *We need to be careful in picking the ones to run with in life.* The Apostle Peter, in speaking of some who had broken with the old crowd, said, "Wherein they think it strange that ye run not with them to the same excess of riot, speaking evil of you" (I Peter 4:4). They had come in contact with a transforming influence which had led them away from ruinous associates. Life with all of its possibilities and opportunities had taken a turn for the better, because of a new influence that was gainful and good, powerful and potent. It has been nineteen centuries since this passage was written, but the problem of human leaven has not changed. There are still people who give us wings to soar and others who encase our feet in leaden shoes.

All of us need an influence that will challenge us, urge us and prod us to do our best. Emerson said, "What I need is somebody to make me do what I can." One of my friends, with great firmness, made a debtor pay the $2,500.00 he owed. Later the man who was tempted to be dishonest said to him, "You are the best friend I ever had. You made me become a man."

● *The Bible issues this warning against going with certain kinds of people:*

> Make no friendship with an angry man, and with a furious man thou shalt not go;
> Lest thou learn his ways, and get a snare to thy soul.
> — Proverbs 22:24,25

And we are told why — lest we learn their ways. So in associating with a person who wields a bad influence, it should be for the purpose of changing him — not to become like him. This spirit guided Christ to become "a friend of publicans and sinners" (Matthew 11:19). If a good man and a bad man go around together, the good man can be made bad, or the bad man can be made good. It depends upon the greater influence!

● *We deceive ourselves if we think we are exempt from outside pressures.* "Be not deceived: evil communications corrupt good manners" (I Corinthians 15:33).

● *Fearful people can fill our hearts with misgiving.* Moses did not want the chickenhearted in his army because of their frightening influence. This was his command: "and the officers shall speak further unto the people, and they shall say, What man is there that is fearful and faint-hearted? let him go and return unto his house, lest his brethren's heart faint as well as his heart" (Deuteronomy 20:8).

The spirit of enthusiasm and victory so radiates from some people that their presence gives you the feeling that you can whip the world. Others have the most depressing effect; and, if you are not careful, you will start thinking the most minor problem is unsolvable. They are defeatists! I must not let their gloom and pessimism rub off on me.

● *A marriage partner's influence can do much to elevate or lower a person.* We are molded by the gospels: Matthew, Mark Luke and John; but there is also the *Fifth Gospel,* the gospel of human influence. The Apostle Peter, in speaking to Christian women, reminded them of what the *Fifth Gospel* could do for their husbands when they had not been moved by the first four: ". . . that, if any obey not the word, they also may without the word be won by the conversation of the wives" (I Peter 3:1). Just as one flower will crowd a home with sweet fragrance, so one life may sweeten a whole family.

The good influence is not only something to receive, but also something to give. In view of this, let each ponder this poetic message:

You are writing a gospel,
A chapter each day;
By deeds that you do;
By words that you say;
Men read what you write,
Whether faulty or true,
Say, what is the gospel
According to you?

BIBLICAL EXAMPLES

1. *Lot* — "dwelt in the cities of the plain, and pitched his tent toward Sodom [and that is where he landed]. But [and this ruins it] the men of Sodom were wicked and sinners before the Lord exceedingly" (Genesis 13:12,13). The result? He lost his family.

2. *Herod* — For his "oath's sake, and them which sat with him at meat, he commanded" that John the Baptist be beheaded (Matthew 14:9,10). If he had dined with a different crowd, perhaps it would have been a different story.

3. *Leaven* — "The kingdom of heaven [the church] is like unto leaven . . ." (Matthew 13:33).

Those who avail themselves of the leaven of the church, will find a purification and stimulation for their lives. The world is bad enough with the church — think how much worse it would be without it!

INFLUENCE NEVER DIES

• *Men die, but their works — never!* Men "rest from their labors; and their works do follow them" (Revelation 14:13).

So when a great man dies,
 For years beyond our ken,
The light he leaves behind him lies
 Upon the paths of men.

— Henry W. Longfellow

• *Death stills man's tongue, but influence gives him another one that speaks forever.* In the Bible it is said of Abel, ". . . being dead yet speaketh" (Hebrews 11:4). A personal question: *What will your influence say of you?*

J

Justice

A BAKER in a little country town bought the butter he used from a near-by farmer. One day he suspected that the bricks of butter were not full pounds, and for several days he weighed them. He was right. They were short weight, and he had the farmer arrested.

At the trial the judge said to the farmer, "I presume you have scales?" "No, your honor." "Then how do you manage to weigh the butter you sell?" inquired the judge. The farmer replied, "That is easily explained, your honor. I have balances and for a weight I use a one-pound loaf I buy from the baker."

This illustrates the injustice of many people. They have two standards: one for themselves and another for the other fellow.

THE EMINENCE OF JUSTICE

● *Justice is one of the lofty qualities God has enjoined upon humanity,* one he has listed in the catalogue of the three great requirements for man: "He hath showed thee, O man, what is good; and what doth the Lord require of thee, but to do justly, and to love mercy, and to walk humbly with thy God" (Micah 6:8)? Justice, mercy, humility and godliness go together, and are essential to the best life.

This trait of fair play — justice — is to God more precious than sacrifice: "To do justice and judgment is more acceptable to the Lord than sacrifice" (Proverbs 21:3). Justice, as we see from the Scriptures, is one of the things worth more than money. It is so necessary to man's well-being and society's goodness that the Bible includes it in the list of things men are commanded to think upon (Philippians 4:8).

● *Justice probes beneath appearances,* knowing that things are not always what they seem. The Bible says, "Judge not according to the appearance" (John 7:24). Surface appearances may be so different from the hidden facts. Taking this into consideration, justice is slow to pass judgment.

Pray do not find fault with the man that limps —
Or stumbles along the road unless you
have worn the shoes he wears —
Or struggled beneath his load.

There may be tacks in his shoes that
hurt, though hidden from view.
Or the burdens he bears placed on your back —
Might cause you to stumble, too.

— Author Unknown

● *Justice never condemns a person without hearing his side of the story.* Justice says, "Thou art permitted to speak for thyself" (Acts 26:1). If you will hear the person, the chances are you will either completely reverse your decision or, at least, alter it.

Judge not! — the vilest criminal may rightfully demand
A chance to prove his innocence by jury of his land;
And, surely, one who ne'er was known to speak his plighted word,
Should not be hastily condemned to obloquy unheard.
Judge not!

— Anonymous

● *Justice never takes bribes,* for gifts blind impartiality. This is one of the earliest recognitions. Moses commanded the ancients: "And thou shalt take no gift: for the gift blindeth the wise, and perverteth the words of the righteous" (Exodus 23:8). The historic Egyptians had a figure which symbolized justice. It was a human form without hands to symbolize that a judge should not take bribes; and without eyes to indicate that a judge of justice should not be influenced by the sight of any person.

● *Justice, having an unbiased heart and open ears, hears and hears again.* This expression of fair play was spoken by some of the Athenians who had just heard Paul's speech at Mars' Hill: "We will hear thee again of this matter" (Acts 17:32).

● *Justice is brave.* Many years ago a man falsely accused was sentenced to die by crucifixion. Public opinion was very pronounced against him. The mob spirit prevailed. He was painfully abused and unmercifully ridiculed as a prisoner. Even in his hour of death he was mocked by his enemies. Many of his friends forsook him. But one man braved the storm of public opinion and "went unto Pilate, and begged the body" and buried it in his own new tomb (Luke 23:52, 53). The crucified man was Jesus. His friend was "Joseph, a counselor; and he was a good man, and a just" (Luke 23:50). Thus it is evident that justice is courageous. It is determined neither by public opinion nor fear, but rather only by that which it believes is right, without fear or favor. The cowards sometimes find themselves in situations where they cannot be just, for they are too afraid to be right.

● *Justice is fair.* It does not have a double standard: one for itself and another for the other fellow. It does not behold the mote in another's eye, while it considers not the beam in its own eye (Matthew 7:3-5). It follows the

Golden Rule: "Therefore all things whatsoever ye would that men should do to you, do ye even so to them: for this is the law and the prophets" (Matthew 7:12).

AM I FAIR?

1. I don't want people talking about me; but do I talk about others?

> Speak not evil one of another. — James 4:11

2. I don't want others judging my motives; but do I judge theirs?

> Judge not, that ye be not judged. — Matthew 7:1

3. I don't want to be defrauded; but do I defraud others?

> Defraud not. — Mark 10:19

4. I don't like to be snubbed; but do I snub others?

> A man that hath friends must show himself friendly.
> — Proverbs 18:24

5. I don't like to be exploited; but do I exploit others?

> Misplaced confidence is like a broken tooth.
> — Proverbs 25:19

6. I like kind treatment; but am I kind to others?

> Be ye kind one to another. — Ephesians 4:32

7. I want honor; but do I freely give it to my associates?

> Render therefore to all their dues. — Romans 13:7

8. I want my acquaintances to accommodate me; but do I show the same helpfulness to them?

> Do good unto all men. — Galatians 6:10

9. When I am sick I want my friends to visit me; but do I visit them in their illness?

> I was sick, and ye visited me. — Matthew 25:36

10. I know a man in business whose conception of fair play and equity is trading with him. Is this my view?

> Look not every man on his own things. — Philippians 2:4

> Be just, and fear not;
> Let all the ends thou aim'st at be thy country's,
> Thy God's, and truth.
>
> — Shakespeare

K

Knowledge

And ye shall know the truth and the truth shall make you free.

— John 8:32

A KNOWLEDGE of the truth, the gospel, frees man spiritually; but this wording is also a great maxim which applies to all aspects of life: *know the truth and be free* — provided you use it. Knowledge is liberty; ignorance is captivity. Let men know the truth of redemption, and they shall walk in the glorious liberty of the sons of God (Christianity is a teaching religion — Matthew 28:19, 20; understanding precedes conversion — Matthew 13:15). Let men learn the scientific facts of the world, and they shall be intellectually free. The great liberator is known and applied truth.

A friend of mine and his associate flew to a small island in the Pacific, inhabited by uneducated, superstitious folk. There they saw a sick old man being soaked in a trough of water. He had been there for days. The witch doctor was trying to cure him by soaking an evil spirit out of him. Ignorance had enslaved them.

Man was once restricted to the old world. Ignorance had limited him. It was knowledge that opened a new world to man. And today it is knowledge that unlocks the gates to new worlds of opportunity, spiritual and material.

Knowledge breaks our chains and cries out, "Now you are free — advance!" Yet it is the voice of caution;

however it is not the tongue that destroys initiative, but rather the voice that gives you confidence to forge ahead!

As a steamer was going up the Mississippi River, a passenger inquired, "Captain, do you know where all the rocks are?" "No," he replied, "but I know where the channel is."

Likewise, it is not necessary that we know where all the pitfalls of life are — there is not enough time to learn them. The important thing is to know where the safe channel of living is and follow its course; for without this knowledge we shall be destroyed. "My people are destroyed for lack of knowledge" (Hosea 4:6). You can never do better than you know!

SOLOMON ON KNOWLEDGE

Solomon, recognized as the wisest man of all times, left for posterity some of the most powerful proverbs on knowledge. The knowledge he discusses, the practical and best, is not merely cognition, but also perception; not merely knowing a thing with respect to its existence and being, but also its excellence and truth. Note:

1. A man of knowledge increases his learning and "shall attain unto wise counsel" (Proverbs 1:5).

2. "Fools hate knowledge" (Proverbs 1:22) — that is why they are fools.

3. "The ears of the wise seeketh knowledge" (Proverbs 18:15) — and that is why they are wise.

4. "The lips of knowledge are a precious jewel" (Proverbs 20:15) — more precious than gold and rubies.

5. "A wise man is strong; yea, a man of knowledge increaseth strength" (Proverbs 24:5).

6. Knowledge is rewarding: it is to the soul what the honeycomb is to the taste (Proverbs 24:13,14).

7. "The excellency of knowledge is, that wisdom giveth life to them that have it" (Ecclesiastes 7:12).

8. There is a type of knowledge described as madness and folly that does not satisfy, but rather increases more sorrow:

> And I gave my heart to know wisdom, and to know madness and folly: I perceived that this also is vexation of spirit.
>
> For in much wisdom is much grief: and he that increaseth knowledge increaseth sorrow.
>
> — Ecclesiastes 1:17,18

Solomon's statement points to a confusion of thought, a wisdom turned into madness and folly, which destroyed all ideas of order and propriety. Solomon further commented, "All is vanity and vexation of spirit." Forgetting God is the acme of folly and the decline of reason which may aptly be called madness. Any learning which leaves God out omits the most essential and practical ingredient of true knowledge. Truly, "The fear of the Lord is the beginning of knowledge" (Proverbs 1:7). If you leave God out, you may learn and learn and the more you learn, the unhappier you become. Intellectualism is not enough! Three cases in point are:

Voltaire, a brilliant literary man of France and an atheist, stated: "Strike out a few sages, and the crowd of human beings is nothing but a horrible assemblage of unfortunate criminals, and the globe contains nothing but corpses . . . I wish I had never been born."

Anatole France, another literary genius but an atheist, said: "If you could read in my soul, you would be terrified . . . There is not in all the universe a creature more unhappy than I. People think me happy. I have never been happy for one day, not for a single hour."

H. G. Wells, one of the most learned and noted men of modern times and an atheist, said in his autobiography: "I cannot adjust my life to secure any fruitful peace . . . Here I am at sixty-five still seeking for peace . . . That dignified peace . . . is just a hopeless dream."

They had knowledge, tragic knowledge! But it was nothing but intellectualism! And that is not enough!

SOURCES OF KNOWLEDGE

The universe is God's University. We are here as scholars learning our lessons, and life is too short for us to be slow learners. In this university we are given five sources for study and personal betterment:

- *The Book of Reason.* "Come now, and let us reason together" (Isaiah 1:18).
- *The Book of Nature.* "The heavens declare the glory of God" (Psalms 19:1,2).
- *The Book of Experience.* "Days should speak, and multitudes of years should teach wisdom" (Job 32:7) — but not always, for some never learn from their experience.
- *Written Books.* The Apostle Paul wrote to Timothy to bring his "Cloak . . . and the books, but especially the parchments" (II Timothy 4:13) — two needs: one for the body and another for the mind and soul; and the need of the latter is so great that sometimes it is better to buy a book instead of a coat.
- *The Bible.* The Book "is profitable for doctrine [teaching], for reproof, for correction, for instruction in righteousness . . . all good works" (II Timothy 3:16,17). No person is well educated who is unlearned in the Bible.

If I would make the most of life — lead myself and others — I must know.

> He who knows, and knows he knows —
> He is wise — follow him.
>
> — Arabian Proverb

L

Love

A BEGGAR at a street corner, with bony hands and pallid lips, asked an alms. The passerby searched his pockets and found that he was without money. Then he took the beggar's hand in his and said: "I'm sorry, my brother, but I have nothing with me." The worn face lighted up, and the beggar said: "But you called me brother—that is a great gift." That is what mankind needs most of all: a love that extends the heart to another and calls him brother. Neither eloquence, nor knowledge, nor faith, nor sacrifice will serve as a substitute for it:

> If I speak with the tongues of men and of angels, but have not love, I am becoming sounding brass, or a clanging cymbal. And if I have the gift of prophecy, and know all mysteries and all knowledge; and if I have all faith, so as to remove mountains, but have not love, I am nothing. And if I bestow all my goods to feed the poor, and if I give my body to be burned, but have not love, it profiteth me nothing.
>
> — I Corinthians 13:1-3, A.S.V.

● *The most essential requirement of a great character is love.* The basic commandments in the Bible concern it: *love God* (Matthew 22:37), *love neighbor* (Matthew 22:39), *love the brotherhood* (I Peter 2:17) *love enemy* (Matthew 5:44). A religion which fancies it loves God when it hates a creature in the image of God is only a self-deceptive malignancy in the heart (I John 4:20).

● *They who give to the world the most love are the most lovely.* Love exhales sweet odors like an open bottle of perfume. Love is so lovely "That they who love are but one step from heaven."—James Russell Lowell. Love's every breath is an inspiration! Its every word a benediction!

BENEFICIAL POWERS OF LOVE

We can no more enumerate the benefits of love than we can count the stars, but here are some:

● *Love is the quality which makes one more like God,* "For God is love." This being true, then "He that loveth not, knoweth not God" (I John 4:8).

● *Love is reciprocal.* A little girl was asked how it is that everybody loves her. "I don't know," she said, "unless it is because I love everybody." She was right! Love begets love. "We love him, because he first loved us" (I John 4:19)

● *Love is understanding*—"love covereth a multitude of sins" (I John 4:8, A.S.V.). This is exemplified most preciously in the life of David. His son Absalom was perverted by hate and misplaced love: hate for father and love for self. Poor Absalom! he wanted to be king and led a revolution against his father. David commanded his officers: "Deal gently [love is gentle] for my sake with the young man" (II Samuel 18:5). But Absalom was killed. And David "was much moved . . . and wept and . . . said, O my son Absalom! my son, my son Absalom! would God I had died for thee, O Absalom, my son, my son!" (II Samuel 18:33). It was easy for the father to forbear because of love. Unless we love and understand people we cannot forbear them—for it is all tied up with love! "Forbearing one another in love" (Ephesians 4:2).

• *Love is a joy-maker.* It is in the realm of the heart—not in the realm of things—that we find the abiding joys of life; and it is there that the sweetest joys are found in loving and in being loved. This is man's nature, for he was created in the image of God who is love; therefore, if man hates, there has been a miscarriage of nature, which understandably makes him restless and miserable. There are no happy, hating people!

In the little village where I grew up it was customary for voluntary workers to dig the graves for the deceased. I recall as we completed a grave, one man looked into it and said, "I wish they were burying me today." Actually he died on the inside years before. Hate had killed him. Bitterness and rancor, restlessness and misery, were his life. They go together!

• *Love will give us courteous manners.* "Doth not behave itself unseemly" (I Corinthians 13:5). It will guard us from trying to have the last word. Actually we should no more fight for the last word than we should struggle for a lighted keg of dynamite.

• *Love is energetic.* The Bible speaks of "labor of love" (Hebrews 6:10) and "faith which worketh by love" (Galatians 5:6). Robert Louis Stevenson said, "So long as we love we serve." Love does not ask how little I can do, but rather how much I can do.

• *Love makes one calmer for the affairs of life,* and in this way better equips him for his business and work. "Love suffereth long" (I Corinthians 13:4).

• *Love will protect man from wronging another* and, in the long run, save him from himself; for he who wrongs friend or foe wrongs himself more. "Love worketh no ill to his neighbor" (Romans 13:10).

● *Love is a necessary condition of the successful and happy life,* for it:

— Smooths the path of duty.
— Wings the feet to travel.
— Pulls the bow which impels the arrow of obedience.
— Winds the mainspring of loyalty.
— Strengthens the arm which tugs at the oar of perseverance.
— Tunes the chords on the harp of life.
— Lays the whole man on the altar of service.
— Puts beautiful rainbows in the black clouds of life.

● *Love will save me frm the waste of life which comes from animosity and bitterness.* This was one of the cardinal principles taught by Jesus (Matthew 5:43,44). I cannot afford to squander life on that which poisons it. No matter how heartless and hateful my surroundings may be, I must refuse to drink the hemlock of hate. There is nothing to gain in snarling back when mistreated or falsely accused. Love—the constructive power of life—will beautify my thoughts, temper my words, mould my motives and inspire my deeds. Life is too short to waste!

There is no time for hate, O wasteful friend,
Put hate away until the ages end.
Have you an ancient wound? Forget the wrong —
Change bitter into sweet; make life a song!

— Adapted, Edwin Markham

M

Meditation

MEDITATE: to contemplate; to ponder; to intend; to plan; to dwell in thought; to muse; to reflect. One of the most essential conditions of a successful and happy life!

For several years I have tried to find some time everyday to be alone and to commune with myself, to search my mind and to tap my soul. I know its value! I found power I did not know I possessed, power I needed so much! and without which I could not have done some of the things I have done.

● *No matter what your vocation is, your most urgent need is to think.* A father, in talking to his son about their business and their big competitors, said, "We shall outthink them." And they have. There is no monopoly on thinking. There will always be a place for the man who thinks. "The man who can't think is a moron; the man who won't think, a fool; and the man who dares not think a slave."

VALUE OF MEDITATION

● *The Bible links the highest and best life with meditation:*

> Blessed is the man that walketh not in the counsel of the ungodly, nor standeth in the way of sinners nor sitteth in the seat of the scornful.
>
> But his delight is in the law of the Lord; and in his law doth he meditate day and night.
>
> — Psalms 1:1,2

> Let the words of my mouth, and the meditation of my heart, be acceptable in thy sight, O Lord, my strength, and my redeemer.
>
> — Psalms 19:14

● *Meditation takes us into the realm of life's issues, our inner nature:* "Keep thy heart with all diligence; for out of it are the issues of life" (Proverbs 4:23) It is there that we become architects of life. Our thoughts make the blueprints. No man will ever be any better or higher than his meditations, the sum of what he thinks.

> For as he thinketh in his heart, so is he.
>
> — Proverbs 23:7

There is power in the mind! in thought! "We can be what we will be, but only by holding ourselves to consistent and well-calculated thought and action. — Sheldon Leavitt.

● *Meditation sharpens our mental and spiritual perceptions and gives us a clearer perspective of life.* This has been exemplified in the lives of many ill people. They were blessed in illness, and for no reason in the world except it gave them more time to meditate and reflect; with nothing else to do, it was easy to "Ponder the path of thy feet, and let all thy ways be established" (Proverbs 4:26)

Eugene O'Neill, who had been a drifter until he was twenty-five, began a new life on a sickbed. It was in the hospital that he first began to write plays.

There was *Florence Nightingale,* bedfast, who did a great work in reorganizing the hospitals in England.

The partially-paralyzed *Pasteur* kept up his attack on disease.

The Apostle John wrote to *Gaius:* ". . . that thou mayest prosper and be in health, even as thy soul prospereth" (III John 2). A sick man with a prosperous soul, and this could not have occurred apart from meditation.

● *Meditation helps man keep his estimate of true values and his sense of proportion.* Since man cannot have everything, he must decide which is the most important. It is as Joshua said, which can be applied to all major principles of living: "Choose you this day whom ye will serve . . . but as for me and my house, we will serve the Lord" (Joshua 24:15).

A decision for one-directional living adds up to personal adjustment and internal peace. This keeps man from being pulled in every direction. His course is set. It is definite, and the result is tranquility of spirit. Halting between decisions is what kills!

● *Through meditation we learn to read the difficult pages in Life's Book.* When pain racks the body and sorrow bleeds the heart, we question, "Why? Why all of this?" But through constructive meditation we come to understand that pain of body and pang of heart, linked with acceptance and adjustment, have done much to sweeten and ennoble human character. The best people I know have been students in at least one of these schools (some in all three): School of Physical Pain, School of Sorrow, School of Disappointment.

● *Meditation helps to guard us from rashness.* Solomon said, "Commune with your own heart upon your bed, and be still" (Proverbs 4:4). Do nothing rashly. Converse with yourself. Sleep on the business.

● *Through musing I may rekindle a fire within me.* "My heart was hot within me, while I was musing the fire burned"

(Psalms 39:3). No matter how gloomy life may be, all hope is never gone for the individual who stops to do some serious thinking.

● *Through meditation we may learn acceptance:*

TO ACCEPT SELF — "Which of you by taking thought can add one cubit unto his stature?" (Matthew 6:27).

TO ACCEPT OTHERS — "And why beholdest thou the mote that is in thy brother's eye . . . ?" (Matthew 7:3).

TO ACCEPT CIRCUMSTANCES — "For I have learned in whatsoever state I am, therewith to be content" (Philippians 4:11).

● *Meditation enables man to dream,* and everybody needs to dream. There he finds hope. There he conquers. There he finds success. There he finds happiness. Have your dreams, and then wake up to make them come true.

● *Meditation affords a release from a too-busy world.* It takes man off the treadmill of hurry, hurry, hurry. It enables him to think soberly, which is one of the commands of the Bible (Romans 12:3). It puts emphasis on direction and safety as well as speed. This helps to bring peace, which everybody wants and only a few have found—many are running so fast they have passed it!

It gives time to think, time to create, time to enjoy, time to explore the deepest part of human nature. It is then that we may discover (I have) some new currents, deep ones, in our inner life-stream. Then we shall have grown a little through meditation and renewal of the inner man. The Bible says, "For which cause we faint not; but though our outward man perish, yet the inward man is renewed day by day" (II Corinthians 4:16).

FINAL EXHORTATION

Finally, brethren,
Whatsoever things are true,
Whatsoever things are honest,
Whatsoever things are just,
Whatsoever things are pure,
Whatsoever things are lovely,
Whatsoever things are of good report,
If there be any virtue,
And if there be any praise,
Think on these things.

— Philippians 4:8

N

No

THE MOST USEFUL WORD

THE editor of a magazine asked a small number of distinguished writers to answer a number of questions, including the following two:

1) In your judgment what word is the most misused?

2) What word in the English language seems the most useful to you?

Nearly all agreed that the most misused word is *Yes,* and the most useful word in the English language is *No.*

Observation has taught us that no one ever amounts to very much or maintains much stature without saying *No.*

We have seen churches torn up, preachers on the move — one there, one coming and one going — because some person or group could not say *No.* Saying *Yes* to pressure groups in any organization eventually brings on problems and headaches galore which can be prevented by saying *No* in the beginning.

Men have passed by fortunes in the pursuit of fortune, all because they could not say *No* to the call of yonder pasture which seemed greener on the other side of the fence. "A rolling stone gathers no moss," but it will not stop rolling until it is blocked with a *No.*

Young people have quit school, hazarded their future, because they could no longer say *No* to money and independence.

Personal tragedy has overtaken many because, in times of weakness and recklessness, they failed to say *No* to evil influences. I went before a judge and pleaded for a young man who had been persuaded to join two others in robbing a supermarket. He got a suspended sentence. Since then he has done idealistically well. The transforming power in his life was learning to say one little word — *No.*

LITTLE BUT BIG

- *This is one of the least but biggest words in the English language.* Little! but so big that only big people can utter it. No man's character is bigger than his ability to say *No.* The biggest man the world has ever known could clearly and unmistakably speak it, while some of his contemporaries could not. His name was Jesus (Matthew 4:1-11).
- *No is the soul's pronounced word of independence.* He who can speak it is master of himself — no man's slave. It gives you the independence to live your own life: determine your own aims, plan your own program, make your own resolutions and proceed as a free man. You are no puppet on a string! Read Acts 5:29.
- *It is the citadel of personal strength* and just as long as a man or woman can pronounce it — meaning it — just that long he or she can remain strong. This was exemplified in the life of Samson (Judges 16). Again, again and again this Herculean man said No! No! No! and his strength remained with him. It was only after his enemies used a woman spy who "pressed him daily with her words, and urged him, so that his soul was vexed unto death; that he told her all his

heart, and" the secret of his strength. Today we have many "Samsons" or giants in character who stand head and shoulders above the run-of-the-mill people, and the only thing that can shear them of their strength is their saying *Yes* to things that correctly demand a *No*. It has protected more women that all the knights of chivalry, and more men than all the armor of the world.

● *This word — No — is the barricade which has blocked the path to millions of young people who were staggering toward the pits of drunkenness and debauchery.* They asked themselves: "Who hath woe? who hath sorrow? who hath contentions? who hath babbling? who hath wounds without cause? who hath redness of eyes?" (Proverbs 23:29). Then they answered: "they that tarry long at the wine . . . At the last it biteth like a serpent, and stingeth like an adder" (v. 32). Not wanting to be bitten and stung, they took Solomon's character-making advice:

> My son, if sinners entice thee, consent thou not.
>
> — Proverbs 1:10

● *It is the latch that bolts the gate to self-respect.* Only those who open the gate by consentment to weakness lose respect for themselves. This is seen in the early history of man (Genesis 3:1-10). Adam and Eve said *Yes* to wrong. Then they were ashamed. Then they hid. When shamed — self-respect gone — the natural reaction is to hide. This has been the pattern of behavior for untold numbers in each succeeding generation — and all because they didn't say *No*.

● *It is the drawn sword that guards the home:* the father from folly, the mother from malefaction, the boys from bad and the girls from gloom.

It was a slave's *No* that protected the home of his master (Genesis 39:7-10). Joseph was the slave. Potiphar was the master. Joseph, young, handsome, talented, was there because he had been sold by his envious brothers. His unusual qualities soon raised him to a place of honor and trust. Then "his master's wife cast her eyes upon Joseph" and tempted him day after day; but he hearkened not, even though appetite and advancement suggested that it was good policy. But principle — not policy — dictated that he maintain his loyalty to his master and his God.

The woman, seeking relief from wounded pride, falsely accused him. It sent him to prison. But he was too big for defeat! With God's help he soon rose to the second highest office in Egypt, next to Pharoah. The turning point in his life was a firm *No.*

- *It is the surest word to reformation.* It challenges the status quo, and only he who can utter it can effect needed changes. The Apostle John could because he was not a *Yes* man. In speaking of Diotrephes' wayward words and dastard deeds, his rejecting some and excommunicating others in the church, John expressed himself in the strongest negative terms and then exhorted, "Beloved, follow not that which is evil, but that which is good" (III John 11) — in other words, say *No* to evil and *Yes* to good. That is the reformative blueprint in any society!

- *It is the voice that balances the parliament of life.* If the *Ayes* always have it, then life is nothing but a Yes-Yes, rubber-stamp existence. The *Naes* must have it part of the time for us to keep our balance of proportion. Pilate, a Roman governor years ago, lost to the *Ayes* because he was too weak to say *No* to a blood-thirty, clamoring mob. He knew Jesus had committed no crime but, for political reasons, he washed his hands in a grand gesture of showmanship, and said, "I am innocent of the blood of this just person; see ye to it" (Matthew 27:24). A *Yes* put his name in the pages of ignominy!

● *No is the only word that gives strength to Yes.* Inasmuch as everything has its positive and negative, then a *Yes* is worthless unless it is backed up by a *No.* You cannot be for something without being against that which is antipodal to it. You can register how loud a man is for something by listening to how loud he utters *No* to that which opposes it. The Psalmist said, "I hate every false way" (Psalms 119:104), which was necessarily true because he loved every true way.

It just works that way. So — it we would make the most of life, we must fortify our *Yeses* with our *Noes.*

Optimism

OLE Bull, the noted violinist, was once giving a concert in Paris when his A string snapped — but he didn't — and he rearranged the composition and finished it on three strings. What courage! What optimism! *Now, that's making the most of life — to have your A string snap and to finish on three strings.*

● *Optimism may be defined as the disposition to look on the bright side of life,* to expect the best, to work for the best, and to believe that the best will come to pass. And reverses which, in time, are sure to come are viewed as only breathers to better prepare one for greater accomplishments. Optimism is the spirit of youth and adventure, which abounds with springtime enthusiasm and newborn resolves, knowing no defeat. It is the spirit of "I can." Paul, the optimist, declared, "I can do all things through Christ which strengtheneth me" (Philippians 4:13). Faith in the unbeatable combination of self-help plus the Lord's help makes for optimism. Turning from the doubts of life, you can find an awakening, a confidence like that of the poet:

> Whichever way the wind doth blow,
> My heart is glad to have it so;
> Then blow it east or blow it west,
> The wind that blows, that wind is best.

But for such optimism to be justified, man has to set his ship's sails to the direction of the wind and send it out. Under-optimism will not let you send your ship out. Over-optimism expects your ship to come in when you haven't sent it out. Balanced-optimism sends your ship out and expects it to come in — that's what keeps the ships going and coming.

RIGHT MENTAL ATTITUDE

● *It is worth more than gold to have the disposition that looks on the bright side of life.* The attitude that the joy of life overbalances the pain of it, that actions and happenings should be interpreted in the light of most favorable expectations, gives one an immeasurable asset.

● *Our cycles of economic depression largely come because of a change in outlook.* Enthusiastic optimism reaches such proportions that pessimistic reactions, with cooling effects, begin and continue until there is a change in attitude. When we reach staggering heights we tend to become afraid; and fear generates pessimism, reason flees, panic develops, and down we come, and down we stay until confidence supplants fear. We have to believe enthusiastically in what we are doing for the world to turn for us. The economic world stopped for the one-talent man because he was afraid (Matthew 25:25). He was a pessimist!

● *The right attitude is the explanation of drive and accomplishment,* as stated in Nehemiah 4:6: "So built we the wall . . . for the people had a mind to work." A mind to do things is the force that built the wall and that builds congregations, church buildings, schools, businesses, cities, and every other thing that is dear to the human heart. Life hands to each a mingled cup; but if you keep the right attitude, you can drink it.

Never give up! for quitting will destroy you —
 Providence kindly, wisely mingled the cup:
Taste the victories and defeats, many and few;
 When the cup's refilled, drink it! Never give up!

— L. B.

REASONS FOR OPTIMISM

1. *Faith in God generates optimism.* We are not permitted to view life's road from beginning to end; we traverse it by faith. "We walk by faith and not by sight" (II Corinthians 5:7). Thus as faith increases, confidence steadies our nerves and directs our steps. It saves us from fainting in pessimism. It did for David who declared, "I had fainted, unless I had believed to see the goodness of the Lord in the land of the living" (Psalms 27:13).

2. *Just to have today heartens us.* As long as there is life there is hope. This optimizes us. Today gives us an opportunity to redeem yesterday's failures. "Redeeming the time, because the days are evil" (Ephesians 5:16). Today gives us another chance! a chance to attain!

Since time began
Today has been the friend of man.
You and Today! A soul sublime
And the great heritage of time.
With God himself to bind the twain,
Go forth, brave heart! Attain! Attain!

— Anonymous

3. *Giving to the world the best you have makes for optimism.* For what you give the world, good or bad, has a way of coming back to you. "For whatsoever a man soweth, that shall he also reap" (Galatians 6:7).

For life is the mirror of king and slave.
'Tis just what you are and do;
Then give to the world the best you have,
And the best will come back to you.
— Madeline Bridge

4. *The fact that every good deed will eventually return to bless its doer invites optimism.* "Cast thy bread upon the waters: for thou shalt find it after many days" (Ecclesiastes 11:1).

5. *The World's Greats teach us to be optimistic.* Many of them — faced with severe handicaps and, in some instances, intractable limitations — accepted their difficulties and, in spite of them, lived life to the fullest. Moses had a speech defect (Exodus 4:10). Joseph was sold into slavery (Genesis 37:23-28). Peter and John were uneducated (Acts 4:13). Paul had a "thorn in the flesh" (II Corinthians 12:7). Franklin D. Roosevelt was a polio victim. Fanny J. Crosby became blind at six weeks of age. But they did not bury themselves in pessimistic self-pity.

6. *It changes life to realize that backsets are often blessings in disguise.* Clouds protect our vision from too much sunlight. So what we need to do is to turn our clouds inside out and see their silver linings.

The inner side of every cloud
Is bright and shining;
Therefore I turn my clouds about,
And always wear them inside out,
To show the lining.
— Ellen Thornycroft Fowler Felkin

7. *Man's cycle of "Ups and Downs" provides an explanation that begets hopefulness.* Scientific research tells us there is a cycle in the rise and fall of emotions. We have read of

the findings of Dr. Rexford B. Hersey of the University of Pennsylvania, which reveal that about every thirty-three days man goes from an *emotional high* to an *emotional low,* and *conversely.* Some days you feel, "You can't keep a good man down"; but other days you think, "You can't raise a good man up." The change is due more to the cycle of internal conditions, the change in glandular functions in which there is a building up and a draining off of energy, than to outside circumstances. So when you are at the very bottom — cheer up — you are ready to turn upward!

P

Prayer

More things are wrought by prayer,
Than this world dreams of.

— Alfred Tennyson

AVAILABLE POWER

THAT'S right! Not just a mere pious sentiment! It is an actual, available avenue to the throne of grace where more has been accomplished than this world has ever realized. It is there that man, stripped of deceit and vanity — for there is no point in trying to fool either self or God — may be his real self and sincerely discuss and earnestly petition help for his frailties and faults, trials and troubles, aims and ambitions.

● *Prayer is every bit as necessary to the vigor of man's spiritual nature as fresh air is to the health of his body.* It is an expression of the inner being, a pouring out of the deepest feelings, a communication of spirit with Spirit, man with God. And that is indispensable!

● *It is an approach to the Father whose ears are open to our prayers* (I Peter 3:12). Jesus used the parental relationship to teach us God's eagerness to grant the request of his children:

> If ye then, being evil, know how to give good gifts unto your children, how much more shall your Father which is in heaven give good things to them that ask him?
>
> — Matthew 7:11

• *Prayer has a double blessing.* In the first place, it helps us to gather together our inner resources — and that is fruitful. "Only in prayer do we achieve the complete and harmonious assembly of body, mind and spirit which gives the frail human reed its unshakeable strength." — Alexis Carrel. Many times we cannot get the courage to stand on our feet until first of all we get on our knees.

And secondly, prayer benefits because God has the ability and skill to answer. The Bible says, "Ye have not, because ye ask not" (James 4:2), meaning *Ye may have, if ye ask.* Thus no human need lies beyond the reach of prayer, because nothing lies beyond the reach of God.

• *Sometimes our prayers are answered differently from our requests* — according to what is best rather than what we think is best — which is all the more proof that they are answered rightly. The Apostle Paul prayed and God replied, but not by giving him what he asked (II Corinthians 12:7-9).

> O sad estate
> Of human wretchedness: so weak is man,
> So ignorant and blind, that did not God
> Sometimes withhold in mercy what we ask,
> We should be ruined at our own request.
>
> — Richard Chenevix French

• *God's answering prayer, of course, is dependent upon our meeting certain, divinely specified conditions;* for instance: address God reverently (Matthew 6:9), pray in faith (Matthew 21:22), be forgiving (Matthew 6:15), be obedient (I John 3:22), pray in keeping with God's will (I John 5:14), and in Jesus' name (John 14:13).

Let us not neglect prayer just because we do not fully comprehend the infinite power of the God at whose throne we kneel. I do not know everything about gravity, but I know it works. Likewise, I do not know everything about prayer, but this one thing I do know — it works. I have learned that from the Bible, common sense, and experience. And that's enough!

HELP IN TIME OF NEED

"Let us therefore come boldly unto the throne of grace, that we may obtain mercy, and find grace to help in time of need" (Hebrews 4:16). We need mercy! We need help! And both are obtainable! So —

1. *If you feel a need for the will of God to be obeyed,* pray — "Thy will be done in earth, as it is in heaven" (Matthew 6:10).

2. If you are concerned about the *need to make a living,* pray — "Give us this day our daily bread" (Matthew 6:11).

3. When you, an erring child of God, feel the *need of forgiveness,* pray — "And forgive us our debts, as we forgive our debtors" (Matthew 6:12).

4. *When there is a need to overcome temptation,* pray — "And lead us not into temptation, but deliver us from evil" (Matthew 6:13).

5. If you *need to escape danger,* pray — "O, let me escape thither . . ." (Genesis 19:20).

6. When life's burdens seem too heavy and there is a *need for rest,* lay them upon God in prayer — "Cast thy burden upon the Lord, and he shall sustain thee" (Psalms 55:22). In this manner, each day's burdens should be laid aside each night. Just as the camel at the close of day kneels to have

his burden lifted, I too as the day draws to a close should bow and let my Master lift the load and grant repose.

PRE-PRAYERED

● *Life is too complicated, too many ups and downs, to be prepared for it unless we are pre-prayered.* Many of the ancient Greats met their problems head-on, because they were pre-prayered.

Nehemiah was prepared to execute his plan to rebuild the walls of Jerusalem (Nehemiah 2:4); the early church was fortified for bloody persecution (Acts 2:42; 8:1); Stephen was strengthened to face death (Acts 7:59); and Jesus was braced for the mob (Matthew 26:36-44) — because they were pre-prayered.

By becoming pre-prayered, we too can appropriate our opportunities, handle our difficulties, and make the most of life. For God "is able to do exceeding abundantly above all that we ask or think" (Ephesians 3:20).

LEAVE IT WITH HIM

The little sharp vexations
The briars that catch and fret
Why not take all to the Helper
Who has never failed us yet?
Tell Him about the heartaches
Tell Him the burdens, too;
Tell Him the baffled purpose
When we scarce know what to do;
Then, leaving to Him our weakness
He surely will see us thru.

— Philips Brooks

Q

Quest

Seek, and ye shall find.
— Matthew 7:7

SEEK

BE active — not passive — if you would find. Don't idly expect the good things of life to find you; go search for them. "Faint heart never won fair lady" — nor anything else. It's not enough to be on the right track. Get going!

● *A passive life is nothing but a piece of driftwood* floating aimlessly down the stream of life, carried withersoever chance directs its course. Such a life accomplishes nothing. It simply cumbers the current. It is in keeping with nature for wood to become driftwood, but it is a miscarriage of nature for man to become driftman. Man was given a mind to think and feet to travel that he may go in quest of what is best and conquer and obtain.

● *God set man's life between its dreams and its tasks when he said:* "In the sweat of thy face shalt thou eat bread, till thou return unto the ground" (Genesis 3:19). Sweat. Work for your bread. Apply yourself. God has not rescinded the law, but rather renewed the urgency of effort in this work-or-starve ultimatum: "If any would not work, neither should he eat" (II Thessalonians 3:10).

The toilsome quest for a larger share
Is wiser than to sit and stare.
Fling forth idle wishes to the wind —
Go after it — you'll make luck bend
In thine own deserving favor.
That gives life a tasty flavor.

— L. B.

● *The world is not built for sluggards.* Nature demands aspiration and quest, or one must suffer the consequences of being a second-rate person.

> Go to the ant, thou sluggard; consider her ways, and be wise.
>
> — Proverbs 6:6

> Slothfulness casteth into a deep sleep; and an idle soul shall suffer hunger.
>
> — Proverbs 19:15

"Every good gift and every perfect gift is from above, and cometh down from the Father" (James 1:17); but not irrespective of man's quest. "The laborer is worthy of his hire" (Luke 10:7), leaving it implied that he is unworthy to receive if he is unwilling to work.

There are good things of God,
They are in store;
Hast thou found some? Give thanks,
And look for more.

● *The road to accomplishment is like any other road: a good place for traveling, but a poor place for sleeping.* Some, however, have gone to sleep at the wheel and need to be waked up lest they destroy themselves. "Awake thou that sleepest" (Ephesians 5:14). Nature says, "Wake up, sleeper, or pull off the road; for you have lost the mastery of yourself."

• *Man's aspirations and quests determine his place in the world.* They did for the one-talent man, the two-talent man and the five-talent man (Matthew 25:14-30). Pulseless men, afraid to climb, can never rise. No ideals stir them, no inspiration fires them, no initiative rebukes their sleepy self-satisfaction. Though they are not really immoral, they are nevertheless wicked. And the one-talent man in the Bible, void of quest, is called a "wicked and slothful servant" (ver. 26). Doing nothing is wicked. So let's be up and doing.

In the world's broad field of battle,
In the bivouac of life,
Be not like dumb, driven cattle!
Be a hero in the strife!
Let us then be up and doing,
With a heart for any fate;
Still achieving, still pursuing,
Learn to labor and to wait.

— *A Psalm of Life*, Longfellow

FOUR KINDS OF PEOPLE

There are four kinds of people:

WISHBONE PEOPLE — they wish for, and long for and sigh, but don't have the get-up to try.

FUNNYBONE PEOPLE — life is a joke and levity blinds the eye; so when accomplishment beckons, they ask sneeringly, "Why?"

JAWBONE PEOPLE — they jaw, rave and cry — long on talk — but short on the try.

BACKBONE PEOPLE — up and at it, they ascend the summits high; for they seek and seek, try and try.

BIBLICAL CHARACTERS WHO SOUGHT

1. *Abraham* wanted peace instead of strife; so he made an unselfish effort to find it rather than wait for it to find him (Genesis 13:8-9).

2. In the midst of a famine, *Jacob* sent his sons to a foreign land in search of food instead of letting them sit and stare at each other (Genesis 42:1).

3. *Jesus* needed transportation; and sent a man to fetch a donkey rather than wait for the donkey to wander there (Matthew 21:1-3).

4. *Zaccheus* sought to see Jesus, but he was short and the crowd obstructed his view; so he climbed a tree (Luke 19:1-4). The lesson is: Don't let the people block your wishes; climb higher and see over them.

5. We are told in a parable of *a merchantman* — could be any one of us — who sought goodly pearls; and when he found one that he wanted, he paid the price to obtain it (Matthew 13:45,46).

Whatever you want, go after it — honestly! and honorably!

SPIRITUAL SEEKING

"Seek that ye may excel" (I Corinthians 14:12) is a command suited to man's spiritual nature. Be not satisfied with mediocrity. Each morning, waking, the soul should feel the urge to rise to the ideal person one ought to be from the person one is; and everyday he should achieve a little more of that image. A big part of the human race is over-bodied and under-souled, because they have not sought first things first (Matthew 6:33).

● *Ideals and quest are transmuted into conduct and character.* They equip man to become a soul-architect who builds his thoughts and deeds into a plan; they lift up life's plodding traveler and compel him forward, not aimlessly, but toward a destination; and for the sailor in life's sea, these two qualities increase the winds and set the sails that he may be driven, not anywhither, but toward a chosen port — guided not by the clouds but by the fixed stars.

● *The secret of man is the secret of what fires him onward.* If this dies, then he is dead, though he keeps on breathing (Revelation 3:1). And earth knows no tragedy like the going out of the flame of aspiration and initiative. But — come what may — as long as it burns, life is worth living.

R

Responsibility

TRAVEL *at your own risk* is the sign you see on some roads. It warns the traveler of his responsibility. The journey of life is similar — each travels at his own risk. I am the responsible party — not others, not circumstances. I have my own life to live, and I am the accountable one for the way I direct it, for my mistakes and failures.

Life's road has its flashing lights of green, amber and red. There are crossroads, and here and there a Y, sharp curves, dead ends, rocks and holes, dust and mud, but I am still responsible for my pilgrimage.

I am the master of my fate;
I am the captain of my soul.

And when I bungle in my journey, *there is nothing to gain in trying to shove the responsibility for misdirection on someone else,* as did my early parents, Adam and Eve. "The woman said, the serpent beguiled me, and I did eat" (Genesis 3:12) — he did it. And Adam said, "The woman whom thou gavest to be with me, she gave me of the tree, and I did eat" (ver. 12) — she did it. But each was responsible! Time could not rub out the deed. What was done was done! And the penalty had to be paid.

● *"You are in charge"* — this was the statement spoken years ago by a merchant in a little country town to his son who was much older than his twelve years. The father was ready to leave on an extensive business trip. He needed somebody in charge who was responsible and trustworthy, and he felt his son met the qualifications better than any other person. The boy had grown up in the business, first working at a candy counter when he had to stand on a box. Now he was twelve and now he was in charge! The other clerks would take orders from him. That son had been grown almost all of his life. It is not surprising that he went on to assume greater responsibilities.

● *Shouldering responsibility is a sign of maturity;* irresponsibility is immaturity. Some people reach maturity in behavior sooner than others: some early, while others it seems never do. Paul said, "When I was a child, I spake as a child, I understood as a child, I thought as a child: but when I became a man, I put away childish things" (I Corinthians 13:11).

"Let George do it!" is the shiftless philosophy of irresponsible people. How much better it would be to volunteer yourself in the language of Isaiah: "Here am I; send me" (Isaiah 6:8).

● *Don't play asleep.* A storm blew up in the middle of the night; and the windows were up in the house where several were staying. A wife punched her husband and said, "Don't you think you should put the windows down?" He whispered, "If we lie still and play asleep, maybe somebody else will." So you can either play asleep or be responsible in life. "Awake thou that sleepest, and arise from the dead" (Ephesians 5:14).

OUR WORLD DEMANDS RESPONSIBILITY

● *Nature shouts, "Be responsible or suffer the consequences!"* To the tree, it says, "Take root and fasten yourself securely or be blown over." And to the river, nature says, "Keep on flowing, for the trees along the bank are dependent upon you; and if you fail them, you will fail yourself, dry up and cease to be a river." David used the tree and the river to teach man his responsibility (Psalms I).

Nature says to the branch in the vine, "Bear fruit or be severed." Jesus used nature's lesson to teach his disciples the responsibility of fruit-bearing (John 15:1-6). Nature is unrelenting in punishing any part of it which fails in its duty. Let man beware!

• *Our world says to man:* "Develop within, perform duties without and exert influences abroad, which are all peculiarly yours, remembering there is no way you can shift responsibility. You can dodge responsibility, but you cannot dodge the results of your dodging."

The Bible spells out this lesson for us in the story of the Prodigal Son (Luke 15:11-16). He could shirk responsibility, but not its penalty of hog-pen living. Life is truly the acceptance or evasion of responsibilities. That's the measure of a man or woman. There is a tremendous debt over every person's head. And payments are demanded:

SOME DEMANDS

Man, an answerable being, is responsible for:

1. *His livelihood* — if he doesn't provide it, he "is worse than an infidel" (I Timothy 5:8).

2. *His way of handling the Bible* — if he adds to it, miseries shall be added to him; if he takes from it, "God shall take away his part out of the book of life" (Revelation 22:19).

3. *His salvation* — "Save yourselves from this untoward generation" (Acts 2:40).

4. *The use of his ability* — more is expected of him who is given more (Matthew 25:14-30).

5. *What he does with his opportunities* — "as we have therefore opportunity, let us do good . . ." (Galatians 6:10).

6. *Keeping his brother* — only the irresponsible ask, "Am I my brother's keeper?" (Genesis 4:9).

7. *Carelessness* — for instance, if he is lax in handling fire that harms another, "he that kindled the fire shall surely make restitution" (Exodus 22:6).

8. *Debts* — "Owe no man anything . . ." (Romans 13:8).

9. *Contracts* — covenants are not to be flagrantly broken (Romans 1:31).

10. *Word* — "Better it is that thou shouldest not vow, than that thou shouldest vow and not pay" (Ecclesiastes 5:5).

11. *Deeds* — "For whatsoever a man soweth, that shall he also reap" (Galatians 6:7).

All of this adds up to the fact that a responsible person makes a living, correctly handles the Bible, seeks salvation, uses his ability, takes advantage of his opportunities, is concerned about others, is cautious, pays his debts, honors his contracts, keeps his word, and watches his deeds.

And what a life this makes!

S

Smile

SMILE! is the motto you see in plants, warehouses, offices and on executives' desks. That which costs nothing is priceless. No man is rich who cannot smile; and no man is poor who can bestow it.

UNIVERSALLY VALUED

There is evidence from every source which establishes the revolutionary and winning effectiveness of a smile.

● *In the first place, the Bible speaks of its power to bless its wearer.* A sorrowful heart which manifests itself in a downcast countenance breaks the spirit of man; but a cheerful heart which shows itself in a smiling countenance lifts the spirit of man. It is a continual feast which feeds him! It is a delightful tonic which doctors him!

> A merry heart maketh a cheerful countenance [a smile]: but by sorrow of the heart the spirit is broken.
>
> — Proverbs 15:13

> He that is of a merry heart hath a continual feast.
>
> — Proverbs 15:15

> A merry heart doeth good like a medicine: but a broken spirit drieth the bones.
>
> — Proverbs 17:22

● *Secondly, business men know the commercial power of*

a smile. A smile may sometimes be very difficult, but it always pays big dividends. Your goods may be better than your competitor's; but if he smiles and you frown, he'll beat you.

The persons I have seen succeed best in life have always been cheerful and hopeful and trod their pathway, whether smooth or rocky, with a smile on their faces. They took the chances and changes of this mortal pilgrimage with a minimun of frowning and grumbling.

● *Thirdly, psychology raises its voice and says, "Smile!"* William James, one of the world's greatest psychologists, says that a smile will produce happiness. So don't wait until your joy bubbles over to smile; go ahead and smile now and a joyful disposition will start developing. Try smiling and you will be happy.

● *Fourthly, Doctors of Physical Health exhort their patients to smile.* Oftentimes they say, "Keep your chin up! Whip this illness with a smile!" A smile is a powerful element of fitness. It is a tonic which protects against the infirmities of ill health. Everytime a person smiles he adds a little to this frail life.

● *Fifthly, the poets portray in beautiful and rhythmic language the force of a smile.*

> But guns and swords and piles of gold,
> Though mighty in their sphere,
> Are sometimes feebler than a smile,
> And poorer than a tear.
>
> — Charles Mackay

● *Sixthly, it is the universal language of mankind.* Though we do not comprehend a foreigner's spoken word, we do understand his friendly smile. It is the window which lets outsiders see one on the inside.

KINDS OF SMILES

1. *Smile of humor.* It is good to be so down to earth that you can see comedy in life. A good story, a bit of banter, a hearty laugh are lubricants which oil life's machinery so that our days have less friction.

Jesus appealed to a sense of humor in presenting the ludicrous in some of his lessons. He gave the case of a man's going to another and saying, "Me thinks me detects a tiny speck in thine eye," while there is a two-by-four sticking out the side of his head (Matthew 7:3). Whimsically incongruous! And Christ told of others who would strain at a gnat and gulp down a camel (Matthew 23:24). Quite humorous! Imagine what a cartoonist could do with these thoughts.

2. *Smile of friendliness.* It is an exhilarating experience to meet someone who smiles and says, "I'm mighty glad to know you." A warm and friendly smile, a radiance like that of the crimsoned dawn, is a magnetism which pulls others to you. It is the key that unlocks hearts. "A man that hath friends must show himself friendly" (Proverbs 18:24).

3. *A smile of pleasantness.* This is the expression of a cheerful disposition. Jesus said, "Be of good cheer" (Matthew 14:27). A pleasant smile injects peace into tense situations, calms tempers and soothes nerves. It is easy for unhappy people to become the source of trouble. They fight with others, because first of all a battle rages within themselves. Pleasantness does not solve all problems, but it certainly makes it easier to solve them.

4. *Smile of courage.* Fear gives you a set and fixed look. Courage permits a smile. It is not the size of a man's physique but the size of his courage that determines his real strength. Being able to smile in the face of dangers which scare others is a tremendous asset. This is half the victory.

David went out to fight the giant Goliath (I Samuel 17). Today all of us have our giants of one sort or another to battle; and as long as you can meet them with a smile, there is still a chance for you.

5. *Smile of mixed emotions.* The Bible says, ". . . concerning them which are asleep, that ye sorrow not, even as others which have no hope" (I Thessalonians 4:11). Hope lets you smile through your tears. Someone has said that no smile is so beautiful as the one that struggles through tears.

6. *Smile of perseverance.* All great persons have beamed in hardships, disappointments and temporary defeats. They just smiled and kept on going: Jesus who was betrayed (Matthew 26:47-50), Joseph who was defamed (Genesis 39:7-23), Job who suffered loss of children and finances (Job 13:15), Gaius who was ill (III John 2), and early Christians who were persecuted (Acts 5:41).

He who smiles — lasts!

IN CONCLUSION: When you smile, another smiles; so why not everyday start something pleasant and helpful?

> Smile, brother, smile;
> When you smile another smiles,
> And soon there's miles and miles
> Of smiles, and life's worth while
> Because you smile;
> So smile, brother, smile.
>
> — Author Unknown

T

Time

AN EXHORTATION TO DAWN

Listen to the Exhortation of the Dawn.
Look well to this day! For it is Life,
  the very Life of Life.
In its brief course lie all the Verities
  and Realities of your Existence.
    The Bliss of Growth;
    The Glory of Action;
    The Splendor of Beauty.
    For Yesterday is but a Dream;
    And Tomorrow is only a Vision.
But Today well lived makes Every Yesterday
  a Dream of Happiness,
  and every Tomorrow a Vision of Hope.
    Look well, therefore, to this Day,
    Such is the Salutation of the Dawn.

TODAY comes only once. It is my day of opportunity. What I do with time as it momentarily comes will completely determine my success and happiness in life's entire struggle. May I not forget that the world was made in six days. If I lose a day, I lose that out of which my own little world is made.

• *One of the prevalent illusions of life is to look upon time as the stale stuff between paydays.* But, really, it's that living vibrant pulse between birth and death, that which cannot be wasted without wasting life, and that which man cannot kill without slowly committing suicide.

● *"On this minute hangs eternity."* These are the inscribed words on a sundial in Harvard Yard. It is there to remind the students of the world's most priceless commodity — time. Every moment trembles with possibilities; every hour is big with destiny.

And if tomorrow shall be sad
Or never come at all, I've had
At least today.
And let no shadow of tomorrow,
Nor sorrow from the dead yesterday
Gainsay my happiness today!

— Yeoman Shield

NUMBER OUR DAYS

Time deals gently with those who use it, but harshly with those who abuse it. "The Road of By and By leads to the town of Never." — Spanish Proverb. "The man who will not execute his resolutions when they are fresh upon him can have no hope for them afterwards: they will be dissipated, lost, and will perish in the hurry and scurry of the world." — Maria Edgeworth.

● *The preciousness of life demands that we "number our days,* that we may apply our hearts unto wisdom" (Psalms 90:12). Though our days are few, we can put a lot of living into them. "For we live in deeds, not breaths, in feelings, not figures on a dial."

He liveth long who liveth well,
All else is but life flung away.

— Horatius Bonar

● *As we number our days, we count up to threescore years and ten,* and by reason of strength on to fourscore years, and by virtue of more strength more years (Psalms 90:10). This tells us that normally we have time enough for accomplishment and happiness — if we use it. So count today and make today count. Not yesterday for it has already been counted. Not tomorrow for when it comes it will be today. The past is not for me. The leaves of the calendar turn only forward. Time's chariot has ratchets on the wheels which permit no turning backward. Yesterday is done. Tomorrow is yet to be. Today is mine! Grab it — not before it arrives nor after it passes, but moment by moment as it becomes the present reality. If I do, then I've learned to live.

> If I take too long to ponder,
> Opportunity may wander.
> Yesterday's a bag of sorrow;
> No man ever finds tomorrow.

● *"Boast not thyself of tomorrow;* for thou knowest not what a day may bring forth" (Proverbs 27:1). This was the tragic error of the rich man in the Bible who let time run out for him (Luke 12:20).

● *"I must work the works of him that sent me, while it is day:* the night cometh, when no man can work," so spoke Jesus (John 9:4).

So — the point of all this is: Take time to live! Make life count! Don't squander yourself!

TAKE TIME TO LIVE

1. *Take time to think* — it is the source of hurnan strength and the measure of a man. Man is the accumulation of his thoughts. "For as he thinketh in his heart, so is he" (Proverbs 23:7). Every person needs some time every day to think. "Ponder the path of thy feet, and let all thy ways be established" (Proverbs 4:26).

2. *Take time to plan* — it is the pursuit of rationality which exercises the mind before working the body. Our purposes should be established by counsel; otherwise, they are sure to be disappointing (Proverbs 20:18; 15:22).

3. *Take time to work* — it is the price of success and happiness. Inspiration without perspiration is a failure. (Genesis 3:19). Take time to work, but don't let work take all your time.

4. *Take time to play* — it is the secret of recreating self. Even Jesus felt the need to walk along a seashore and to go into the mountains.

5. *Take time to read* — it is the foundation of knowledge. The man who doesn't read has no advantage over the man who can't read. Reading makes life full, significant and interesting; it provides help for many problems and a refuge for many miseries. Above all, read the Bible some every day (I Timothy 4:13), and then translate the reading into life itself.

6. *Take time to be friendly* — it is the disposition that makes friends (Proverbs 18:24).

7. *Take time to assist others* — life is too short to be selfish. Philippians 2:4.

8. *Take time to weep* — it is the outlet of deep feelings which need to be expressed. "Weep with them that weep" (Romans 12:15).

9. *Take time to laugh* — it is the medicine for the heart. "A merry heart doeth good like a medicine" (Proverbs 17:22).

10. *Take time to be thankful* — it is the sure way to make your state look different. "Be ye thankful" (Colossians 3:15).

11. *Take time to investigate* — it is better to be safe than sorry. One of the compliments in the Bible was paid the Bereans because they investigated (Acts 17:11).

12. *Take time to serve God* — it is the conclusion of the matter and the whole of man's duty (Ecclesiastes 12:13). And when death comes and cuts off time, he is then ready for eternity — and another world. What a life! What a future!

U

Unselfishness

MANY years ago some robbers held up a traveler, took his possessions, beat him and left him half dead by the side of the road. By chance another man came along, but he did no more than look at him and pass by on the other side. And another traveler came, looked and continued his journey. No doubt each reasoned that it was not his problem, none of his business and he could not take the chance of being entangled in trouble. But a third man came whose heart was moved with compassion. He doctored the victim's wounds, took him to an inn and cared for him through the night; and the next day when he left he made financial provision for the innkeeper to continue the care.

Here are some observations: Selfishness mistreated the man. Unselfishness treated him. We see the causative forces of evil and good in our world — selfishness and unselfishness. One creates the trouble while the other effects the cure. The selfish ones took and had less, for it made them smaller. The unselfish one gave and had more, for it made him bigger.

This is the story Jesus told in teaching a lesson on neighbors (Luke 10:30-37). He made it plain that we have a moral obligation to be neighborly toward all people who need our aid and assistance — and it is predicated on unselfishness, a basic requirement of good behavior, happiness and success.

A BASIC REQUIREMENT

1. *The second commandment of the law* requires: "Thou shalt love thy neighbor as thyself' (Matthew 22:39) — unselfishness.

2. *The Golden Rule* demands: "Therefore all things whatsoever ye would that men should do to you, do ye even so to them" (Matthew 7:12) — unselfishness.

3. *Pure and undefiled religion* necessitates that we "visit the fatherless and widows in their affliction" (James 1:27) — unselfishness.

4. *Doing "good unto all men,"* as we have opportunity, demands — unselfishness.

5. *That which refines and beautifies man* requires: "Look not every man on his own things, but every man also on the things of others" (Philipians 2:4) — unselfishness.

6. *One of the outstanding qualities in the admirable life of the Apostle Paul,* the man who wrote much of the New Testament, is aptly expressed: "And I will very gladly spend and be spent for you" (II Corinthians 12:15) — unselfishness.

7. *One of the factors in Jesus' greatness* is thus revealed: "The Son of man came not to be ministered unto, but to minister" (Matthew 20:28) — unselfishness.

8. *The secret of eminence for us* is found in one simple and brief statement: "And whosoever will be chief among you, let him be your servant" (Matthew 20:27) — unselfishness.

9. *"It is more blessed to give than to receive"* (Acts 20:35) — unselfishness.

So if we would make the most of life, let us philosophize and pray:

O Lord, I pray
    That for this day
I may not swerve
    By foot or hand
    From thy command,
Not to be served, but to serve.

For therein is accomplishment and satisfaction; all else is vanity and vexation.

THE SELFISH

● *He who receives but does not give is as stagnant and unattractive as the Dead Sea.* All the fresh waters of the Jordan River cannot enliven and refresh its dead salt depths, for it self-devotedly receives and never gives. It hoards and never shares. Its own self-absorption has consigned it to death — the Dead Sea. Comparatively, all the streams of God's bounty cannot animate and invigorate a heart that has no outlet, one that ever receives, but never overflows and gives. Like the Dead Sea, such a self-centered existence is only a Dead Life.

That man may last, but never lives,
Who much receives, but nothing gives;
Whom none can love, whom none can thank, —
Creation's blot, creation's blank.

— Thomas Gibbons

● *"No man can live happily who regards himself alone,* who turns everything to his own advantage. Thou must live for another, if thou wishest to live for thyself." — Seneca. The self-clinging person is miserable; and that's the reason — he's all wrapped up with himself.

O I could go through all life's troubles singing,
Turning earth's night to day,
If self were not so fast around me clinging,
To all I do or say.

— Frederick William Faber

• *The unduly selfish person is incapable of true friendship,* for friendship cannot be a one way concern. He will exploit you. He is your feigned friend as long as he can make capital of you. He is like some who sought Jesus for the loaves and fishes (John 6:26). He will use you to help him financially, to climb socially, to enhance his image, to aid his family, or to satisfy his egotism. But if you need help, then you find out that he is no friend — just an exploiter.

• *The self-absorbed individual has a weak character.* He blows from either the east, the west, the north or the south, depending upon his varied self-interests. He plays both sides of every street and works both ends against the middle. The stuff he feeds you is hard to stomach — when you learn him; for it is too thick for a spoon and too thin for a fork. He is brave when there is no fight. For the sake of opportunism or vengeful satisfaction he may secretly knife at your back, because he is too cowardly to fight you openly at your face. His decisions are not made on the basis of right and wrong, but primarily on the grounds of how they will affect him, though he pretends a selfless interest. "For a piece of bread that man will transgress" (Proverbs 28:21). He longs to fill big shoes; and when he gets the chance, his own selfishness — which begets envy — shrinks him to such littleness that he can barely see out. What a shame!

THE UNSELFISH

I know no great men and women except those who have

given themselves to the betterment of others. The secret of their bigness is found in their bigness of heart.

- *The unselfish are more:*

  — *Humble.* Selfishness makes one proud.
  — *Forgiving.* There is less wounded pride.
  — *Sincere.* Not controlled by selfish motives.
  — *Hospitable.* There is an interest in others.
  — *Charitable.* There is a feeling for others.
  — *Tolerant.* Can see another's viewpoint.
  — *Friendly.* Makes for the outgoing spirit.
  — *Joyful.* Happiness comes from helping others.
  — *Adjusted.* Adjustment is easier when one forgets self.
  — *Beautiful.* Pretty is as pretty does.

This table looks like a list of love's qualities, and rightly so, for love "seeketh not its own" (I Corinthians 13:5). Love is unselfish!

V

Vision

Eyes have they, but they see not.

— Psalms 115:5

THAT is the explanation of many failures in life. Eyes that cannot see!

Some people are blind. Though they look, they never see. And the trouble with some others is — their eyes are in the back of their head. But one forward view is worth a thousand hindsights.

There are so many wonderful things in life for man — glorious occasions, lucrative opportunities, worlds to conquer — if he has the vision to see them. See! Don't just look! For he who outsees others can outlive others.

Good vision gives you the perspective of a new world, which sees the Everywhere, with great possibilities up ahead. The beneficial vision is the fine art of foreseeing something big come from that which seems little and inconsequential — *this is seeing opportunity.* Further, it is the power to apply the principles of deduction which flows from impartial comparison — *this is discernment.* And further, it is the ability to see with independent ideas — *this guards one from the blind rut of prejudice.* And still further, it is the faith which sees the unseen — *this gives power to see a new beginning for life's every ending, and this we call hope.*

VISION CAN GIVE YOU ANOTHER WORLD

There is *an old Indian legend* about a father and his three sons. He pointed to a high mountain many miles away and ordered the youths to climb up the mountain as far as they could and to bring back a memento of their adventure. One returned with an unusual flower. The second came back with a rare rock. The third returned and said, "I climbed to the top and I brought back a vision of the sea." That is the most important of all; for if you have the vision, you can cultivate the flowers and quarry the rocks. In this particular case, it led them to build canoes and sail to a more fruitful and habitable island. With no vision their lives were a restricted existence.

When *Columbus'* crew threatened to take his life and turn back, he swore that he would show them land if they would wait a few more hours. Before the time expired, land appeared on the horizon. Was it luck? Not at all. It was the recompense of a great strength coupled with a brilliant observation. He had noticed bits of grass floating upon the waves, and he knew they could not be far from the land that grew the grass. Discovering a new world was not a stroke of luck, but rather the culmination of vision, courage and observation, accompanied by heroic efforts. These are the roots of all great achievements!

● *Jesus was the most visionary man the world ever knew.* His vision embraced the whole world for the sake of the world. He said, "Go ye into all the world and preach the gospel to every creature . . ." (Mark 16:15,16). That is vision! The kind that will provide a new world!

SEE OPPORTUNITY

The Bible says, "As we have therefore opportunity . ."

(Galatians 6:10). But it takes vision to see it. *For we make luck by seeing opportunity.* Luck seldom calls on those with closed eyes.

Charles Goodyear suffered many disapointments in his experiments to make rubber usable. Once as scoffers ridiculed him, he threw a handful of the sticky gum mixed with sulphur on a hot stove. When he attemtped to scrape it off, he found that it had charred. He had made weather-proof rubber. It has been cited as one of history's most famous accidents. *But Goodyear maintained that the incident had meaning only for the man "whose mind was prepared to draw an inference."* That's vision!

● *Fortune seldom comes to any except the visionary.* No one can honestly say, "I've had hard luck all my life." There was good luck ahead, but he failed to recognize it; if so, it seemed so far beyond his reach that he wouldn't shorten the distance by stepping toward it. Vision is valueless, if it is unaided by a moving courageous aspiration.

SEE TO DISCERN

The Bible talks about having our *"senses exercised to discern both good and evil"* (Hebrews 5:14). To do this, one needs the insight to see beyond appearances.

In another Indian story, the Big Chief held out an acorn and asked his son what he saw. The son replied, "An acorn." The father continued, "Where you see an acorn I see an oak." This principle of perception should be applied to all the affairs of life. The world has its good and bad; and the ability to distinguish one from the other, especially in its embryonic state, is a most needed and practical insight. There is where Adam and Eve failed. They had the short view (Genesis 3:6).

SEE WITH UNBIASED EYES

Jesus said, ". . . their eyes they have closed, lest at any time they should see . . ." (Matthew 13:15). Prejudice had closed their eyes and put them in a rut. But it is easy to see the truth when there is no commitment to error.

General Lew Wallace is a classic example. In preparing to write Ben-Hur, he made an earnest study of the Bible. He said: "I was in quest of knowledge, but I had no faith to sustain, nor creed to bolster up . . . my vision not being clouded by previously formed opinions, I was enabled to survey it without the aid of lenses. I believe I was thorough and persistent. I know I was conscientious in my search for the truth. I weighed, I analyzed, I counted and compared." In going from conjecture to knowledge and from opinion to belief, he said,". . . at length I stood firmly and definitely on the solid rock . . . convinced . . . of the divinity of the lowly Nazarene who walked and talked with God." — *Little Visits With Great Americans,* Marden, pp. 303, 304.

It was this vision that ennobled the *Bereans* and handed them down to immortality (Acts 17:11).

SEEING THE UNSEEN

• *It is through faith that we see the unseen.* This was the vision of Moses of whom it was said: "By faith . . . endured, as seeing him who is invisible" (Hebrews 11:27). This never-to-be-forgotten man of history could see a new world, opportunity and even the unseen.

So — get your eyes open! and fortune will favor you!

W

Work

And the Lord God took the man, and put him into the garden of Eden to dress it and to keep it.

— Genesis 2:15

In the sweat of thy face shalt thou eat bread.

— Genesis 3:19

THESE passages take us back a long way, to the Garden of Eden and to one of the first established rules of human conduct. The centuries have proved it to be one of the greatest laws of economics, and of health, and of happiness; so much so that it cannot be violated without destroying the individual and society. It is the law of existence! It is the rule of betterment for the whole man — body, mind and soul!

A REQUIREMENT OF SUCCESS

A young man applied for a job in a small factory. The owner, being supplied with workers, said, "I am sorry, but we don't have enough work to keep another employee busy." The applicant replied, "I am sure you have. You don't know what a little bit of work it takes to keep me busy." The young man was already walking the road of failure, for he was violating a divine injunction. One of the laws of God is: You can't get something for nothing—not for long. Nature's ultimatum is: Work or fail!

• *By learning to work we have a better chance of being successful.* Yeoman Shield expressed it in this unique manner:

THE SUCCESS FAMILY

The father of Success is Work.
The mother of Success is Ambition.
The oldest son is Common Sense.
Some of the other boys are: Perseverance,
Honesty, Thoroughness, Foresight, Enthusiasm,
Cooperation.
The oldest daughter is Character.
Some of the sisters are: Cheerfulness, Loyalty,
Courtesy, Care, Economy, Sincerity, Harmony.
The baby is Opportunity.
Get acquainted with the "old man" and
You will be able to get along pretty
Well with the rest of the family.

● *One of the great success stories of all times* — the rebuilding of the Jerusalem walls — is explained in only eight words: "For the people had a mind to work" (Nehemiah 4:6).

● *Work is included in the Biblical list of three things essential to success:* "And that ye study to be quiet, and to do your own business, and to work with your own hands, as we commanded you" (I Thessalonians 4:11).

— Be quiet — not noisy.
— Mind your own business — not the other fellow's.
— Work with your own hands — don't expect handouts.

● *The Bible presents three objectionable alternatives to work:*

— Work or beg. "I cannot dig; to beg I am ashamed" (Luke 16:3).

— Work or starve. "If any would not work, neither should he eat" (II Thessalonians 3:10).

— Work or steal. "Let him that stole steal no more: but rather let him labor" (Ephesians 4:28).

There is no comfort in the Bible for lazy folk. Christ himself was a carpenter. Paul was a tent maker.

● *These divine and human proverbs* focalize the urgency of work, if man would succeed:

> Go to the ant, thou sluggard; consider her ways, and be wise.
>
> — Solomon, Proverbs 6:6
>
> He also that is slothful in his work is brother to him that is a great waster.
>
> — Solomon, Proverbs 18:9
>
> The desires of the slothful killeth him; for his hands refuse to labor.
>
> — Solomon, Proverbs 21:25
>
> Good times are just ordinary times made good by hard work and thrift.
>
> — L. B.
>
> Through planned work man sets his sails to favoring breezes.
>
> — L. B.
>
> Working at the job beats carrying a rabbit's foot for luck.
>
> — L. B.

A REQUIREMENT OF HEALTH

● *Employment is nature's physician.* Health requires sleep, contentment, food, water and exercise. But if you will meet the latter requirement, the others will come naturally.

I learned this when I was sixteen. Another young man and I went to a German settlement to thresh grain. They spoke German. He and I spoke English. But hard labor, hungry appetites and exhaustion, shared together, are universal languages. They often give a deeper understanding than words can convey. The days were the longest in the year and we worked from dawn to twilight; the bundles of grain were heavy; and the Texas sun was radiant hot. We ate at the cookshack and slept on the ground. By my present standards, the food was sloppy and the bed was hard; but, really, there have been only a few times since when I have found food so good and sleep so sweet. And that well water — there has never been any better. It was then that I learned, "The sleep of a laboring man is sweet" (Ecclesiastes 5:12), though I did not know that was a verse in the Bible.

● *If you quit work, health may quit you.* Idleness allows the mind to imagine a thousand ills. Keeping employed will help to keep the mind; and keeping the mind will help to keep the body. Though you may retire from employment for financial gain, never quit work. Never!

A REQUIREMENT FOR HAPPINESS

● *The happy life does not come at half price.* No amount of cheating or bargaining will obtain it. Pay the going price or be denied it. The full cost demands a full life — and that includes work! The parasite never knows paradise.

A few years ago the principal of a large high school made a study to see how many of the pupils like to work. He learned one very interesting thing, that the boys and girls who liked to work got the most satisfaction and delight in life. They were the ones that the future would be sure to favor with more success and happiness.

● *Idlers have more disturbances and discords than workers.* This is Bible: "For we hear that there are some which walk among you disorderly, working not at all, but are busybodies" (II Thessalonians 3:11). Busybodies! produced by unfulfillment and frustration, grown in the devil's ugly field of idleness! Doing nothing is a hard row to hoe, described by Solomon as "a hedge of thorns" (Proverbs 15:19).

X

Unknown

AFTER miles of smooth going in the pursuit of noble purposes in life's journey, one suddenly comes upon this sign, *DETOUR!* Now life's traveler, disturbed, stares in a state of uncertainty and hesitation. He did not plan on this. It can't be so, but it is! Not being able to run the barricade, there must be an adjustment and a change of plans. Now he must leave the good road for the rough one where traveling is difficult and laborious. But every detour, after a certain amount of turns, bumps and dust, leads to the main highway which oftentimes is a better road than the one traveled beforehand.

LIFE'S UNKNOWN VICISSITUDES

- *Prosperity and adversity* are counterbalanced:

> In the day of prosperity be joyful, but in the day of adversity consider: God also hath set the one over against the other, to the end that man should find nothing after him.
>
> —Ecclesiastes 7:14

For the good of man, the wise Creator has balanced prosperity and adversity against each other. God has arranged the curriculum in the school of life to the end that man may lack nothing when school is out — provided he is a good scholar. Some pass; others fail. And that too is life!

I have walked down Skid Row in New York City and beheld the victims of life's troubles. The rug had been pulled

pulled out from under them in one way or another — by themselves or someone else. But in each case there had been an action and a reaction: an action which hurt the individual and his own reaction which hurt him more.

● *But what pulled some down to Skid Row has lifted others up to Success Row.* The difference was not in the experience but in the reactions. Severely tried, they proved to be "more than conquerors" (Romans 8:37). Like the crushed flower that gives a sweeter odor than the untrampled one, adversity sweetened their lives. Some, in facing their perplexities, have confidently echoed the faith of Job who said, "When he hath tried me, I shall come forth as gold" (Job 23:10). Later they looked back and appraised their troubles in the language of David: "It is good for me that I have been afflicted" (Psalms 119:71).

● *"My burden has let me see the stars."* These are the revealing words of a minister who for years has borne the ordeal of a back-breaking personal problem. He could have permitted his load to bend him head-forward and low, and he could have seen nothing but the dust at his feet. But he chose to try to stand erect, and the weight bowed him backward and focused his view into the heavens — and he saw the stars! and the darker the night the brighter they shone!

● *Adversity need not shackle us.* Luther translated the Bible into German while incarcerated in Wartburg Castle. Bunyan wrote Pilgrim's Progress in Bedford jail. Madame Guyon's sweetest poems were the results of her long imprisonment. Paul wrote some of the New Testament books while imprisoned. Each so adjusted as to prove that there is a part of man that cannot be bound. Truly, "Stone walls do not a prison make, nor iron bars a cage."

• *Loss of health may give a deeper insight and a broader outlook.* Franklin D. Roosevelt was struck down by polio. The unexpected immobilized him, but it did not keep him from moving into the White House. Suffering no doubt mellowed his famous Fireside Chats.

• *Ridicule may fire one to success or burn him to a crisp.* "What will this babbler say?" (Acts 17:18) was hurled at the Apostle Paul, but it did not deter him. When E. Stanley Jones started to preach his first sermon his mind went blank. As he prepared to sit down in despair, a girl's giggle put fire into him.

• *Though slander hurts at the time, it doesn't have to kill.* It's the holding of post-mortems that brings on the effects of death. Joseph did not let slander down him. A look at his life proves that we should not try to read the message of distress through the envelope in which it comes (Genesis 50:29).

• *The loss of a loved one bleeds the heart, but a resignation to the unchangeable heals the wound.* It did for Job who said, "The Lord gave, and the Lord hath taken away; blessed be the name of the Lord" (Job 1:21). Resignation does not prevent weeping; but that, too, can be helpful. It is sometimes easier to see when the eyes have been washed with tears.

TRIUMPHANT QUALITIES

Great people who successfully handled the unexpected and the unknown had these qualities:

1. *Self-inspection.* When the apostles were told that one of them would betray their Master, each asked, "Lord, is it I?" (Matthew 26:22).

2. *Courage.* Peter and the other apostles gave this answer

to their persecutors: "We ought to obey God rather than men" (Acts 5:29).

3. *A disposition to pray.* In meeting their opposition, Nehemiah commented: "Nevertheless we made our prayer unto God" (Nehemiah 4:9).

4. *Work.* The widowed Ruth gleaned in the fields (Ruth 2:3).

5. *A forgiving spirit.* Jesus prayed for his enemies: "Father forgive them; for they know not what they do" (Luke 23:24).

6. *A spirit that returns good for evil.* Saul admitted this greatness in David: "Thou hast rewarded me good, whereas I have rewarded thee evil" (I Samuel 24:17).

7. *Faith and perseverance.* Job, who suffered loss of children, health and wealth, said: "Though he slay me, yet will I trust in him" (Job 13:15).

8. *Adjustment and determination.* David, who lost his son in death, stated: "Wherefore should I fast? can I bring him back again? I shall go to him, but he shall not return to me" (II Samuel 12:23).

CONCLUSION

● *Dire necessity adds strength and color to life by awakening the sleeping giant within us.* In the tropics in Africa a traveler came upon a large butterfly struggling to free itself from the cocoon. In his misguided mercy the wayfarer set it free. But when freed from struggle, it lost its brilliant coloring. So it is with man: The beautiful colors of the soul are won in the exertion with and in the triumph over adversity. "By these things men live" (Isaiah 38:16).

Y

You

YOUR life is up to you!

Each can say:

> I am the master of my fate:
> I am the captain of my soul.
>
> — *Invictus*, William Henley

A young man, seeking help, came into my office. His clothes were soiled, but more than this — his soul. He showed many signs of a hard life. The world had been unkind to him, but he had been unkind to the world; he had violated its demands, and it had assessed its penalty. A pitiful sight was he. He had sown and he had reaped: from his drinking he had reaped debauchery; from his idleness, poverty; from his riotous living, broken health; and from his vagrancy, friendlessness. *"For whatsoever a man soweth, that shall he also reap"* (Galatians 6:7). A law of God and a law of nature. He had sown wild oats and had reaped an abundant harvest that already had an overcrowded market; so there was no demand for him — in his present condition.

This is what I told him: "You have unmade yourself; now if you are ever remade, you will have to do it — with God's help. In the last analysis, every person is self-made or self-unmade. Oh! circumstances and other persons enter in, but the real making or breaking is due to self.

"You and your past — whatever it was — you made it; you and your present — whatever it is — you are making it; you and your future — whatever it will be — you will make it.

"Our hands can supply some needs for you; our ears can listen for some opportunities for you; our tongue can guide you; and our heart can pray for you — and all of this we shall gladly do — but if you ever advance, you will have to do the walking.

"I have talked and you have listened, but that's not enough; you will have to do the doing. 'But be ye doers of the word, and not hearers only, deceiving your own selves' (James 1:22). That's individual responsibility. No one can assume it for you. Life can be no better for you than *you* make it. You need to *come to yourself,* and maybe you have. *Be yourself. Do your best. Be a man.* It's up to you!"

Yes, he made progress.

COME TO YOURSELF

- *Only by coming to yourself can you better yourself.* The Prodigal Son never made progress until he came to himself (Luke 15:11-24). He saw himself where he was and where he would like to be; and without blaming anybody he traveled the distance between the two. Whether you are a prodigal or not, if you want to get somewhere there has to be a beginning and a direction: the beginning is where you are and the direction is where you want to be — so get going!

- *The Prodigal Son's living a riotous life and later a hog's life were both out of character for him.* He had learned his lesson. He just wanted to be himself again.

BE YOURSELF

● *You cannot make the most of yourself unless you are yourself.* This does not bar improvement (Hebrews 6:1). But the improvement should be made as yourself — not as somebody else. In speaking of himself, Paul said, "I am what I am" (I Corinthians 15:10). He recognized his own individuality where — and only where — growth was possible.

● *You can be yourself; but you can never be anybody else.* To try to be somebody else is to be nobody; because there can be only one of a person and duplicates don't count. The person who tries to be somebody else is a double failure: he is neither himself nor the other fellow; he is a fraud.

● *"To be natural;* to be yourself; to be original; to be independent; to stand four-square against all opposition that would thwart a worthy purpose, is the mark of high *individualism* . . . God . . . gave each person a brain with which to think, and failing in this, individuality goes by default." — Dickson.

● *Each creature is the greatest success in being its natural self.* It is natural for the eagle to soar and for the donkey to bray. But if the eagle should attempt to bray and if the donkey should try to fly, there would be a comedy of failures.

Preposterous? No more so than many of the people who pose and strut in unnaturalness. There is no success for any person in trying to be a peacock or a parrot. It is a great privilege just to be yourself. Therein is the secret of greatness and happiness. What has been called big and little works are misnomers. All work, whether following the plough or leading the people, is great if it's natural and one's best. That is the universal democracy of success.

That puts it within the reach of every individual. All you have to do is be yourself and do your best.

DO YOUR BEST

• *Responsibility demands that you do your best* — response to ability. God requires this, but no more (Matthew 25:14-30).

> That man is blest
> Who does his best
> And leaves the rest
> — to God.
>
> — Adapted, Charles F. Deems

BE A MAN

• *Here is a test of maturity:*

1. A mature person is *not afraid to try* for fear he will fail (Matthew 25:14-30).
2. A mature person *will work* — not find an excuse for indolence (Proverbs 22:13).
3. A mature person *has faith in himself* (Philippians 4:13).
4. A mature person *is persistent* (Luke 9:62).
5. A mature person *blames himself* — not the other fellow — for his mistakes (II Samuel 12:13).
6. A mature person *is reasonable* (II Thessalonians 3:2).
7. A mature person *is never too proud* to do the little things (Luke 16:10).
8. A mature person *is temperate* (II Peter 1:6).
9. A mature person *is too big to be little* (Genesis 50:15-21).
10. A mature person *is not childish* (I Corinthians 13:11).

Z

Zeal

A business friend of mine said, "There is no substitute for brains; but if there could be, it would be zeal." That's how important it is.

A NECESSARY QUALITY

• *Solomon commended the zealous spirit in these words:*

> Whatsoever thy hand findeth to do, do it with thy might.
> — Ecclesiastes 9:10

• *Zeal is faith in action;* and faith without initiative is powerless (James 2:16). But when man's faith is coupled with action, he climbs mountainous barriers and forges ahead of the laggards.

• *Zeal is unmistakable evidence that you are whole-hearted in what you are doing.* No matter what other qualities are yours, if you are short on this one — zeal — you will find yourself on the losing side of life.

• *The winners have kept the torch of enthusiasm burning* when the losers allowed the flame to die into the cold dark night of despair. Men of enthusiasm lead the way. Without enthusiasm no battle has been won, no book written, no skyscraper built, no business expanded, no wilderness inhabited and no religion propagated.

• *Zeal ranks ahead of money and influence.* Wealth and prestige will unquestionably open some doors, but it is enthusiasm that pursues the opportunities. Fervor overwhelms and overpowers all obstacles. It spurns inaction, tramples prejudice and storms indifference. Single-handedly the enthusiast convinces and dominates where a multitude of unenthusiasts can scarcely raise an eyebrow of interest.

• *Zeal is the explanation of many a success;* for instance, the rebuilding of the crumbling walls of the ancient city of Jerusalem:

> So built we the wall; and all the wall was joined together unto the half thereof: for the people had a mind to work.
>
> — Nehemiah 4:6

That's why they raised that wall! zeal!

After running the gauntlet of youth, after taking the blows of nature and the harassments of the severe critics, if there is still enthusiasm in the twenties — look out — there is a life with a future. So keep the flame of enthusiasm burning in your religion, business and social activities. It will warm cold blood, inspire cooperation and effect results beyond your fondest dreams.

IT TAKES BOTH

Success in business and church demands both knowledge and zeal. Take away one and you ruin the other. Zeal without knowledge is runaway energy; and knowledge without zeal is useless.

The inadequacy of some is due to *zeal without knowledge* (Romans 10:2).

The trouble with others is *knowledge without zeal* (Revelation 3:15,16).

Knowledge gives direction. Zeal provides the push. Put them together and you have a winning combination.

THE DEVELOPMENT OF ZEAL

Just to talk about the essentiality of enthusiasm is not enough; so let us consider some ways to develop it.

- *In the laboratory of human experience there is nothing more creative of zeal than a rapturous sense of God,* who is:

OMNISCIENT....................."Thou knowest my downsitting and mine uprising thou understandest my thought afar off." Psalms 139:2

OMNIPRESENT ...."Whither shall I go from thy Spirit? or whither shall I flee from thy presence?" (Psalms 139:7). Being Spirit, he is not limited by time or space.

OMNIVISUAL...................."Yea, the darkness hideth not from thee; but the night shineth as the day: the darkness and the light are both alike to thee." Psalms 139:12

OMNIFIC.........................."I will praise thee; for I am fearfully and wonderfully made." Psalms 139:14

OMNIPOTENT ...."Marvelous are thy works; and that my soul knoweth right well." Psalms 139:14

These reflections give us hope; and as hope increases,

zeal grows. As we come to know God, the scales drop from our eyes and our vision lengthens, our trust broadens, and our zeal sparkles. Yes, a thousand perplexities may loom up before you; but just do your best and trust Him for the rest; and you will find a thrill in the day and a tranquilizer in the night. Truly this is what man needs!

- *A look at our world should provide a spark of intensity.* "Lift up your eyes and look on the fields" (John 4:35). For it is an arena of infinite promise. It is a marvelous world, full of sublimity and possibility, responsive to man's development. It is full of meaning, waiting for man to dig it out. It is an endless adventure, calling man from here to there. No one can sense the universe — and its meaning — without experiencing a thrill that sweeps the soul.

- *Others are a basis for enthusiasm,* because man needs man — and has man. Most people are basically good and are so constituted that they are ready to "Rejoice with them that do rejoice, and weep with them that weep" (Romans 12:15). In the road ahead, when the emergency arises, the Good Samaritan will step forth with the helping hand. You will be surprised at how many are willing to "Bear ye one another's burdens" (Galatians 6:2).

- *A realization of the powers of self inspire zeal for living.* God has endowed me with an intellect like his own. "God created man in his own image" (Genesis 1:27). I am not a weak worm of the dust, but the crowning work of creation. I am the product of infinite genius. Because of man's unusual capacity, he was given charge of the world. This means that I should develop this philosophy in my inner consciousness:

— I am God's Masterpiece.

— I am important to God and to his plan for the *now* and the *hereafter*.

— I can grow.

— I can be useful and that is greatness.

— I can build a road that leads to the everywhere.

— There is always a way through.

— Nothing is too good to be true.

● *It stimulates zeal to know that we can all succeed in what matters most* — and that is how we play the game. Whether we win, draw or lose — according to faulty standards — is not nearly as important as the character developed in the struggle. For when commendation and condemnation fall upon ears that cannot hear, how we played the game is the only thing that will count.

For when the One Great Scorer comes
  To write against your name,
He marks — not that you won or lost —
  But how you played the game.
— Grantland Rice